Abel
emerging

a reconsideration of the christian story
for a sustainable world

Ron Rude

BEAVER'S
POND
PRESS

ISBN 10: 1-59298-313-8
ISBN 13: 978-1-59298-313-1

Library of Congress Catalog Number: 2009940545

Printed in the United States of America

First Printing: 2010
Printed on 30% recycled paper

14 13 12 11 10   5 4 3 2 1

Cover and interior design by James Monroe Design, LLC.

Beaver's Pond Press, Inc.
7104 Ohms Lane, Suite 101
Edina, MN 55439–2129
(952) 829-8818
www.BeaversPondPress.com

To order, visit www.BeaversPondBooks.com
or call (800) 901-3480. Reseller discounts available.

To Nancy for her encouraging love,

Jen for her inspiration,

and Angela for her steadiness.

To Leigh —
Towards sustainable
and faithful living.

Ron Rude

Contents

Fear less—Hope more

Eat less—Chew more

Whine less—Breathe more

Talk less—Say more

Hate less—Love more

—John Fisher (1848–1920)

I don't wish man in control of the universe.
I wish nature in control, and man playing only his just role
as one of its inhabitants.

—Randy Morgenson, 1971

Introduction

The Christian story needs to be reconsidered. That is the premise of this book.

To say this implies that there is something inadequate about current considerations. It suggests, and I know this is presumptuous, that the dominant versions of the old, old Christian story that we have known and loved so well and for so long, as well as the wildly innovative and contemporary incarnations that have shaped Christianity in recent decades (including those currently lighting up the blogosphere, Twitter, and YouTube), in large measure fall short. After nearly 2,000 years of meandering and compounding through the centuries and cultures of history, the greatest story ever told, as it has now been deposited at our feet in our time, is not only weak when compared to what it has to offer, but also insufficient to the task of meeting the daunting challenges of our time.

These are strong statements. One might ask, So what is inadequate about our current rendition of the Christian story? My answer is this: it has grown small. What is the remedy? It needs to find its larger truth again.

One example of this "smallness" has to do with anthropocentricism. That is, the story has become merely about *Homo sapiens*. I propose that finding our larger story involves a recovery of and reconciliation with the wider community of life, from vegetation and animals to reptiles and bacteria, from landscapes and oceans to rivers and air. Bringing the insights of theology and science together, especially evolutionary biology, palaeoanthropology, and Earth science, I will try to begin this process.

Another aspect of this "smallness" predicament involves loss of potency. At the start of the twenty-first century, the vessel of life called Planet Earth is listing toward calamity. Members of *Homo sapiens* are doing the damage, scientists and others tell us. Humanity's voracious appetites are overconsuming biomass, reducing (oversimplifying) diversity, depleting freshwater supplies, poisoning the atmosphere, deteriorating precious soil, fouling the oceans, and extinguishing other species of life at alarming rates. Why are humans behaving this way? Why do we seem so unable to stop, so unable to self-regulate our overindulgences? And why are we members of *Homo sapiens* who are Christian (and this includes me) doing as much damage as anyone? Yes, it is true. Though commendable anecdotal accounts can be found, on the regional and macro level, followers of Jesus of Nazareth and Jesus the Christ are no different than anyone else when it comes to destroying God's creation. We too are conducting our lives poorly. Why is that? What have we Christians not understood about our own seminal story that has made our message so destructive on the one hand, and so impotent to bring hope on the other?

So far I've used the word "story" seven times in this brief introduction. I could have used "narrative" or "myth" and meant the same thing. The repetition is intentional and implies significance. An individual's or family's story shapes how the generations in that family system will unfold. The founding and accumulating narrative of a culture or nation shapes the worldview, values, and destiny of that culture or nation. Even a species' myth—of how it came to be, its place vis-à-vis the wider community of life, its relation to the Creator, its own self-understanding—shapes how that species will understand itself, and thus, how it will behave. Humans enact stories. That's what humans do. How we mold and fashion those stories will determine how we live in God's world. And how we live in this world will determine our impact, for good or ill, on this place that is home to this treasure called life. Stories are indeed that consequential. In short, stories matter.

In 2008, I was drawn to an unfolding horse-racing drama that captivated much of the equestrian world. After stunning victories at the Kentucky Derby and Preakness Stakes, thoroughbred superstar Big Brown was predicted to gallop away with an easy victory at the Belmont Stakes in New York State. Attaining such a goal would be a remarkable achievement, making this extraordinary stallion the first race horse in a long while to win the prestigious Triple Crown. To win in this manner would launch an enthralling legend that would capture the hearts of millions and spawn numerous books and movie deals. It would also, no doubt, make a few people rich. "A foregone conclusion," his able trainer boasted. The bookies lined up. The crowds gathered. The day was set. But then something unexpected happened. On the day of the race, jockey Kent Desormeaux had to ease Big Brown up on the home stretch. To everyone's horror, the champ could barely find his stride. He sputtered. He stammered. He strolled in in last place. "There was no energy, no run. I had no *horse*," Desormeaux lamented afterward, in front of the cameras, in bewilderment.

In the following chapters, I propose that current versions of the Christian message have no horse. I do that as a Christian. I do this as one who is searching to reclaim the truths of Jesus of Nazareth and Jesus the Christ.

I remember taking a religious studies course in college on the apostle Paul. On one particular day, the professor, Dr. Jack Clark, was trying to get us to notice the audacity of Paul's claim to certitude. We noticed; how could we not? It was especially apparent when Paul proclaimed to the church in Galatia, "I am astonished that you are so quickly deserting the One who called you in the grace of Christ, and are turning to a *different gospel*—not that there is another gospel" (Galatians 1:6–7a, emphasis added). Apparently Paul was worried. He went on, "Even if we, *or an angel from heaven*, should proclaim to you a gospel contrary to what we proclaimed to you, let that one be accursed" (1:8, emphasis added). Hmm. This did sound serious. And later, when referring to those persons who would pitch another gospel, he invoked his own graphic preference that they "would castrate themselves" (5:12). Yes, we noticed Paul's audaciousness all right, as words like "bold," "rash," and "arrogant" flew like Frisbees during our classroom discussion. But we also wondered, what was Paul getting at?

I've pondered this very question for years. This book is an attempt to make clear one possible answer. It is formulated in the context of the multitude of profound crises currently confronting our world, coupled with a sense that there is something inadequate, even amiss, about the Christian message that is supposed to offer transformation, healing, and hope. This book is written for all those who may share those concerns.

At the start of the twenty-first century, Planet Earth is in grave distress. Humans are the species doing the damage. It is my view that the current dominant versions of the Christian story are the engine driving this destruction, at least in Western cultures. It's not just imperfect practices that are doing the damage, but the story itself. Through its sometimes uplifting and sometimes harrowing two-thousand-year journey through history, this narrative has been usurped and domesticated too many times by the powers and principalities of church, commercialism, politics, fundamentalism, warfare, and even household. It has lost its effectiveness, its vitality, its verve. As such it has become *the* reason we are unable to steer a better course. In other words, what Christianity has become through its circuitous journey may be the thing about which St. Paul warned so earnestly in his own time.

There are, of course, others who have also been suggesting such "heresies." It's what Brian McLaren is getting at in his book *Everything Must Change*. Everything. It's part of the message of

Barbara Brown Taylor in *Leaving Church,* John Shelby Spong in *Why Christianity Must Change or Die,* Shane Claiborne in *The Irresistible Revolution,* and Richard Heinberg in *The Party's Over.* I especially commend to you the remarkable writings of Daniel Quinn, including *Ishmael, The Story of B,* and *Beyond Civilization.* These and other helpful books are listed in the bibliography. They all speak with a sense that something has gone profoundly awry.

Of course, some scientists, politicians, religious leaders, corporations, educators, and even households are trying to turn things around. They see the burgeoning population growth, local and global pollution, species extinction, retreating glaciers, deforestation, and are rightly alarmed. Efforts at change are sincere and noble, and exhibit a grasp of the many complex issues that come together to yield these problems. But those efforts are doomed to failure, I believe. Why? Because there is a force at work greater than all these efforts combined. That force is a deeper, cultural/religious narrative. This story is the air we breathe and the airwaves that persistently engage, shape, entertain, and numb us. It is the ethos that establishes our assumptions and the pathos that makes us blind to our presuppositions. Unless this narrative is exposed, dismantled, and actually replaced with a truer version and vision, scientists, politicians, religious leaders, corporations, educators, and even households will have little chance of offering a ripple of true hope, let alone of turning an intractable tide.

It will be best to dive right into these pages. I trust you will experience a fair number of lightbulb moments. That is my intention, anyway. Hopefully, the pieces of the montage will give way to a larger picture as this alternative narrative unfolds.

But along with diving in deep, you will also need a higher lookout perch to see this larger picture unfolding. Imagine standing with your feet squarely on the ground and looking back at the horizon. You see the near distance, but you can't see beyond the line where the Earth meets the sky. Now imagine climbing a tall telephone pole. From this vantage, you begin to see a new middle distance materialize, revealing additional terrain as well as a new and more distant horizon. Now climb a towering California redwood. Hanging in the wind at three hundred and sixty-five feet, you begin to see a landscape of greater depth and breadth you hadn't known existed. Finally, summit a small mountain peak. Each time you look back, the horizon recedes farther back in time, revealing a farther and wider distance in a growing and more complex panorama. Heretofore unknown peoples, places, and events start becoming part of a larger story. The vista expands. Your perspective changes. Back stories and sidebars begin to suggest new meanings to previous understandings of the world and your place in it. A bigger, more complete chronicle unfolds.

This book invites you to come atop that small mountain peak. In so doing, you will begin to see a longer, grander, and more truly historic narrative than has probably been included in your previous considerations. This larger narrative includes many fascinating ideas, some of which are the following:

- Earth life is ancient and evolving (rather than young and finished).

- Death is part of life (rather than a curse or punishment).

- Life on Earth thrived prior to the emergence of humans (rather than found its purpose in our recent arrival).

- Members of *Homo sapiens* are created in the image of God *and* in the image of all other Earth creatures (we forget either at our peril).

- Humans are scouts, trailblazers, pioneers (not the end product or crown of creation).

- Humans are surrounded by and an integral part of an evolving garden of life (not separate from, superior to, or the reason for this garden).

- The biblical story of the Fall refers to an event/concept that is recent (rather than original).

- The Fall story refers to a new human claim to exceptionalism (rather than to an arbitrary act of personal disobedience, a loss of species innocence, or the ending of a time of former garden bliss).

- Life under Cain's rule (as opposed to God's) brings destruction (as opposed to blessing).

- Sin and destruction is Cain's inevitable nature (not humanity's).

- Cain's story must find its demise (rather than be tweaked or fixed).

- Abel's story must emerge (before it's too late).

- The Creator is ever-evolving the Earth with greater variety and complexity (not destroying it).

- Jesus Christ, and perhaps other religious figures, came with a mission to heal Cain and his legacy (not affirm Cain's worldview and behavior, or offer Cain a salvific escape from the consequences of his worldview and behavior).

- Earth is humanity's home (not a disposable way station on the road to an afterlife or heaven).

- There is hope (but not in the short term).

Anatole France (1844–1924) wrote, "What is traveling? Changing your place? By no means. Traveling is changing your opinion and your prejudice." This is a travel book. It is a voyage of the heart and mind and foot. Its goal is simple and presumptuous: to change human hearts and worldviews in order to immediately and ultimately change the practice of both faith and life among our species. This must be done to save the world.

Some may find the destinations of this journey to be heresy, if not nonsense. If this is the case, feel free to brush off these ideas like dandruff. Others like me, though, will find in these thoughts and their staggering implications the bigger story for which our souls have long been hungering.

Here is a brief tour of the book's contents:

Part I proposes a reframed creation narrative. It embraces the notion of an evolving Tree of Life and discards the ideology of human exceptionalism.

Part II describes the emergence of evil as one aspect of an aberrant human culture that subverted God's intentions, pursued world dominance, and achieved world dominance.

Part III is an intermission. It addresses questions and objections evoked by the material presented in parts I and II.

Part IV tackles the question, Is there hope? The answer proposed is yes, but not in the short term. As an antediluvian proverb wisely notes, "If the road is one hundred miles into the woods, it is one hundred miles out of the woods."

Part V is a bold reconsideration of the Christian story/message/claim. It tackles current understandings of Christianity and proposes a distinctive and grander narrative.

Part VI calls for a new direction and way of living.

Before beginning, a word about footnotes. You will discover footnotes at the bottom of many pages. I invite you to see them not simply as required citations or tedious distractions. Rather I invite you to see them as treasures. They will send you into many fields besides theology, including Earth science, evolutionary biology, palaeoanthropology, astronomy, and history. My intention is to show how God's incredible world is integrated into a marvelous whole. Everything breathes into everything else. You will also find a bibliography at the end of Part VI. These marvelous books have helped educate me in fields other than my own. And finally, appendix D offers group discussion questions for each chapter.

These pages contain theology, certainly, though framed in ways perhaps new to you. They also contain current insights from science that I have found fascinating, and I hope will fascinate you too. And because I am a passionate and concerned person, these pages will also occasionally include my two cents worth of social commentary and critique.

I have felt the stirrings of this book for some time. Though I serve as a Christian minister and truly love Jesus, I am definitely an iconoclast and am uncomfortable with much that falls under the banner of Christianity. The works of three authors—Daniel Quinn, Desmond Tutu, and Michael Pollan—have provided a major catalyst in shaping my journey. Daniel Quinn, whom I have already mentioned, helped me see the extent to which certain understandings of the stories of Adam and Eve and Cain and Abel have historically and negatively shaped not only Christianity, but also western civilization. He has assisted me in thinking differently about the Bible's creation and Fall stories, and especially about the character Abel, who though overlooked, murdered, and forgotten by the church and world, was the one who lived a life favored by the Creator! I'll explore the "why" of that favor and employ this parable as a kind of background template throughout the book.

I have also gained deepened understandings of theology from the life and writings of Desmond Tutu, especially his book *No Future Without Forgiveness*. His insights underscore the crucial linkage between forgiveness and relationship, and will help to shape the closing chapters.

Finally, I am grateful for the works of Michael Pollan. His remarkable book on food, farming, economics, and culture—*The Omnivore's Dilemma: A Natural History of Four Meals*—is a must read for anyone serious about the implications of our industrialized food systems.

So how does one reconsider the Christian story, as well as Earth's story and humanity's story? How does one find an alternative version of a narrative that has so shaped our understandings of God, this life, and this world? To do this, and to rediscover an incredible and unfolding epic, we go back to the beginning.

—Ron Rude
www.abel-emerging.com

Part One
The Creation Story Reconsidered

Chapter 1
Ancient and Evolving Rather Than
Young and Finished

Long, long ago, perhaps trillions and trillions of eons far distant, the Creator embarked on a journey of creation. Splashing seasonings of flavor and cacophonies of sound in all directions, the master chef and song-maker conceived and created, envisioned and unfurled, bursting forth with creative genius, wild delight, and promise. We can't even imagine the vastness of this creation. A scientific theory called "string theory" even proposes the existence of countless universes besides our own. Why might the Creator's domain be so vast?

A shorter time ago, approximately 13.7 billion years back, our own particular universe began to come into existence. Pure energy at the start, the stirrings of this universe took 500 million years or so to cool down sufficiently so that particles and atoms, the building blocks of matter, could come together. This matter spread out in grand patterns to create billions of galaxies, each containing billions of stars and planets. How large did this universe become? This expanding universe became so large that, traveling at the speed of 186,000 miles per second (or 670 million miles per hour, or 5.87 trillion miles per year), a phenomenon called light requires nearly 13.7 billion years to stretch from beginning to current end. Again, why the immensity? Why the extravagance? And why did God begin to create in the first place?

And about 4.6 billion years prior to today, the Creator began to fashion the home we know and love and are dismembering, this striking orb called Planet Earth.

Earth began as an ember, a speck of debris erratically orbiting a blazing star we call the sun. This rowdy, elliptical path eventually smoothed out—except for a slight wobble. This wobble, similar to the quivering of an automobile's tire when it is out of balance, journeys through a full wobble cycle approximately every 40,000 years, creating greater and lesser distance, timing, and intensity of solar heat hitting Earth. A scientific theory by Milutin Milankovitch (1879–1958), known as the Milankovitch cycle theory, ties this grand-scale shimmying, along with the tilt of the Earth on its axis and Earth's changing orbital shape from round to oval, to the periodic coming and going of Earth's Ice Ages.[1]

As time went on, this relatively small ember, though active with erupting volcanoes, searing lava, and the constant bombardment of heat-producing meteors, cooled. Volcanic gases emitted from the Earth's depths. These gases combined to form numerous compounds. One such compound was H_2O, or water. It is most likely that most of the building blocks for this water came from sources within the Earth, but a scientific theory called "panspermia" suggests that some of Earth's compounds—like H_2O—may have arrived aboard comets and asteroids that crashed onto Earth's surface prior to the forming

1.   There have been twenty-three Ice Ages since about 2.5 million years ago. The Wisconsin glaciation (corresponding to the Würm glaciation in Europe) is the most recent, ending around 11,000 years ago.

of its protective shield of atmosphere, magnetic field, and ozone. But however it came to be, water proved particularly essential to Earth's impending experiment with life, generating a global chain reaction of humidity, moisture, and the unleashing of centuries and centuries and oceans and oceans of rainfall.[2]

And at some point along Earth's planetary journey, about 3.8 billion years ago, chemistry evolved into biochemistry and biochemistry into biology, and a phenomenon called "life" began to emerge in its many embodied forms.[3] Again, organic compounds most likely emerged from hydrothermal vents deep within Earth's ocean floor. However, an additional theory suggests origins from outer space. The Murchison meteorite (named for the Australian town where it was discovered in 1969) contains traces of sugar and amino acids. These are both organic compounds that are part of the building blocks of life.

Life is a mystery. What is it? Though hard to define, those things with life do things like use energy, breathe, eat, grow, eliminate, reproduce, and evolve. Living things also die, making space and place and fertilizer and energy for the spawning of

---

2. Today, salty seas account for 97 percent of our planet's water. Salinity rates vary. The Dead Sea (bordering Jordan, the Palestinian West Bank, and Israel) has an approximate 25 percent salinity rate; Utah's Great Salt Lake, 17 percent; the Mediterranean Sea varies from 4 to 6 percent; and the Atlantic and Pacific Oceans, 2 to 5 percent.

    The remaining water on Earth, approximately 3 percent, is freshwater. Of that 3 percent, two-thirds is required for maintaining ice caps, permafrost, and glaciers, or lies too deep under the ground to access. Therefore, only 1 percent of Earth's H_2O is actually available freshwater. This must sustain all land life and all creatures that inhabit and depend on freshwater lakes and rivers.

3. A word about datings; they vary. For example, scientists generally calculate the origin of the universe at 13.7 billion years, while others reason dates of 15 to 16 billion years ago. The same is true for the emergence of single-cell life (or crustaceans, or mammals, or primates, or *Homo sapiens*). The scholarly world of scientific journals and peer-reviewed papers is extremely intricate, and beyond the abilities of the layperson to master. Also, as hypotheses are tested and new evidence deduced, conclusions rightfully alter. For the purposes of this book, when dates and timelines are indicated, I have chosen what currently appears to be the most widely accepted hypotheses, with the recognition that these datings often change as scholars, scientists, and others consider more research.

new life. The gift (in my interpretation) of life may very well exist on countless other planets in God's universes. But certainly it exists in abundance and splendor on this tiny sphere.

As time went on, God's Earth evolved into an ocean and sky and eventual garden of aliveness, a wild and ample ecology generating numerous and assorted species. Simple life forms evolved into more complex life forms. Single-celled creatures developed into algae, polyps, protozoa, jellyfish, and amphibians.[4] Sea life moved onto land. Land life transformed into bacteria, fungi, plants, and trees. Invertebrates such as insects, worms, and Lacewing butterflies emerged, as did vertebrates such as dinosaurs, reptiles, tiny and large mammals, insect- and nectar- and seed-eating birds, and primates. The Tree of Life (I will use this phrase to refer to any and every thing that is involved in change and variation, including the physical world, the subatomic world, the chemical and biological world, and the world of mind and spirit) bustled and flourished in a heady mix of rich, Earthy fragrance. Every species evolved on the path of life. Never a finished product, each species changed and adapted to ever-changing and ever-adapting ecosystems. Ancient life evolved into a splendorous display of wonder and diversity. That life continues to evolve today.

---

4.   The oceans reach astonishing depths, including 36,198 feet in the Marianas Trench near Guam. Photosynthesis (a process that uses sunlight to drive a chemical reaction that turns CO_2 and H_2O into sugar and creates O_2 as waste) takes place to about 500 feet, and some light is detectable at 3,000 feet. Below 4,000 feet there is absolutely no light, and total darkness reigns.

Chapter 2
Alive, Not Utopia

While adjectives expressing amazement will never be sufficient to describe the richness of creation, it should be noted that God's garden was never intended to be utopia. "Utopia" (Greek: ou-τόπια) literally means "no place." "No place," by definition, has never existed. Rather, God's garden was *alive* from the start. And it was varied. And sustainable. As such, it contained the provisions of life in its entire relational and interdependent splendor: birth, death, thunder, lightning, rainfall, wind, volcanoes, seasons, Earthquakes, hurricanes, bacteria, viruses, sex, termites, conductivity, sunsets, parching drought, raging floods, forest fires, fungi, mosquitoes, snow and ice, youth, middle age, old age, uplift and erosion, weather patterns, photosynthesis, and evaporation. The garden of life was a carnival of robust and thriving delights.

Of course, there were many conditions that governed the evolving aliveness of God's garden. There was and is a *food chain*. All species get their nourishment from other species, and that has been the Creator's, as well as nature's, way. However, very few species kill except to eat or in self-defense.[5] When hungry, a lion will kill and consume an antelope. But when the lion is full, the antelope can literally nap a short distance away. Richard Heinberg describes the concept further:

> At first ecologists studied food chains—big fish eating little fish. Quickly, however, they realized that since big fish die and are subsequently eaten by scavengers and microbes that are then eaten by still other organisms, it is more appropriate to speak of food cycles or webs. Further analysis yielded the insight that all of nature is continually engaged in the cycling and recycling of matter and energy. There are carbon cycles, nitrogen cycles, phosphorus cycles, sulfur cycles, and water cycles."[6]

There also was and is *balance* in the garden. If the birthrate of lions soars, then an excess of antelope gets eaten and the antelope population decreases. This will soon cause starvation among some of the lions until balance asserts itself again. If the antelope birthrate soars, the increase in food supply will allow for more lions to be born, which then grow up to eat more antelopes until the antelope population goes down enough to restore balance. This balancing act of life and death occurs simultaneously on hundreds of thousands of levels and stages, with incredible complexity and terrifying responsibility. Again, consider these words from Heinberg:

---

5.   Food chains and food cycles are fascinating to study. Certainly there are species that kill for more than food or self-defense. Mantis insects, for example, kill competitors during the mating cycle. Others kill to defend their offspring. Viruses kill to reproduce. And some wolverines and apes have been known to sporadically kill for no apparent reason (at least to us). Yet to conclude, therefore, that this is nature's way, and that God's community of life is all about killing others before they kill you, is misleading. Such data can be manipulated to excuse a hostility-based worldview and violent approach to living.

6.   Richard Heinberg, *The Party's Over*, 15.

In climax ecosystems, population levels are kept relatively in check not only through predators culling prey species, but also through species acting on their own to limit their numbers via internal feedback mechanisms. These internal mechanisms are seen in elephants, for example, which regulate their population densities through delays in the onset of maturity as well as among smaller animals such as mice, where females typically ovulate more slowly or cease ovulation altogether if populations become too dense. In many bird species, much of the adult population simply does not breed when there is no food-energy available to support population growth.[7]

But thankfully, the Creator perceptively and compassionately guided these intricate systems from deep within the chambers of the Creator's domain, a jurisdiction symbolized in the Hebrew scriptures by the Tree of the Knowledge of Good and Evil (Genesis 2:9). This balancing act flowed out from within the Creator's domain, and was the work of God, and God alone.[8]

One might think this is unfair—leaving the governance of the universe, including Planet Earth, to the Deity. After all, who was God to set the rules? Why should God be the one to establish which creatures live and which die, one today and tomorrow

---

7.   Ibid., 17. It should also be noted that while some species have feedback loops, others (such as rats) do not.

8.   I'm aware that some may disagree with my choice to introduce a Creator figure into this story of life, especially one portrayed as a being who is involved in life's evolving journey, and who has attributes like "terrifying responsibility," "perceptive guidance," and "compassion." While I elect this portrayal, I know it is scientifically unverifiable (as is God's existence—though God's nonexistence is equally scientifically unverifiable). It must be admitted that just because the Bible says God exists or acts in a certain way doesn't mean that God exists or acts in a certain way. What it does mean is that the writer(s) believed God existed and acted in certain ways based on the writer's understandings and perceptions of certain internal and external experiences and concepts. Does this mean all God language is subjective? Yes. Does this mean everything having to do with God is scientifically unverifiable? Yes. Does this mean that one can speak of reality only in scientific terms, that indeed science captures the full scope of reality? In my view, no.

another? Perhaps such management could be improved upon. Perhaps some created species rather than the Creator could do a better job of ruling the Earth.

But alas, this was and is not possible. God is the Creator, and the Creator is God. No other species or creature was or is God. The relative fairness or unfairness of life in the garden resides under the Creator's care and management for the good of all.[9] God alone has the authority, goodness, and wisdom symbolized by the Tree of the Knowledge of Good and Evil, and God alone can handle its terrifying power. No species has, or ever will have, such ethical stature or spiritual and intellectual aptitude.[10]

And so, the Creator's imagination and care (dare we say love?) continued to unfold a world of diversity and splendor for eons, often in stunning episodic bursts of transformation, mutation, and change. Under the reign of God, encoded and enfleshed into the laws of nature, the Tree of Life evolved and flourished. No creature was any more important than any other; all were needed. Nor was the creative process intended for the benefit of any one creature over the others.

---

9.   I also assert (equally nonprovable) that the Creator interacts with Creation in profound though ambiguous ways, as the one in charge, though not the controller.

10. God commanded all creatures to keep their hands off the Tree of the Knowledge of Good and Evil, "for in the day that you eat of it you shall die" (Genesis 2:17). Such severe responsibility is beyond the capability or stature of any creature, including humans.

   **Note: It is not my intention to offer biblical "proof-texts" for my claims, or to give the impression that quoting a verse can capture the deeper message of God's story. When I use an occasional biblical quotation, understand that it is meant to help us think about Earth's story, humanity's story, and God's story differently.

Chapter 3
In the Image of God *and*
the Other Creatures

At some point in the creative process and within the community of life, approximately 3 to 4 million years ago, a certain strain of primates emerged.[11] Over hundreds and thousands of generations, this strain evolved into a species called *Australopithecus*. We recognize this as a predecessor species to *Homo sapiens* (current humans). Living resourcefully in the garden in relative accord with the Creator's implanted wisdom, *Australopithecus*, over the course of many, many more generations, evolved into *Homo habilis*. The word *habilis* means "handy" or

---

11. There are currently 250 known primate species, 75 of them found in Brazil. The evolving pathway of hominids (current humans and our predecessor species) diverted from the evolving pathways of many other primates about 7 million years ago. Currently, the five closest primates to *Homo sapiens* are the gibbon, orangutan, gorilla, bonobo, and chimpanzee. We share between 98.4 and 99.2 percent identical genetic material with chimpanzees.

"skilled," referring to the use of tools and various hand capabilities that require memory, advanced planning, the ability to work out abstract problems, and the communication of knowledge. This species also lived in good complement with all other creatures for hundreds of thousands of years, later evolving into *Homo erectus,* or "upright man." Members of this species, like their predecessors, migrated into various regions of Earth. And ages later, approximately 200,000 years before our time, *Homo erectus* evolved into the current but transitory form of that species, *Homo sapiens,* with modern *Homo sapiens* (also called *Homo sapiens sapiens* because of our ability to think symbolically) perhaps evolving some 130,000 years later.[12] The Swedish botanist, physician, and biologist Carl Linnaeus (1707–1778) coined the name *Homo sapiens,* which means "wise" and "able to apply knowledge," though it is becoming more apparent that these traits apply to other species as well.

Why do all species, including primates, continue to evolve? In this reconsideration, the successful evolving of any species, including humans, is as much a matter of survival of those species that "fit in"—who by instinct or conscious action abide by the conditions of the whole community of life and of God's transcendent and immanent governance—as it is "survival of

---

12.   This summary is admittedly simplified. In general, *Australopithecus anamensis* (found in Kenya) dates back 4 million years, *Australopithecus afarensis* ("Lucy") 3.2 million years (becoming extinct 1.4 million years ago), *Homo habilis* 2.5 million years, and Homo erectus 1.6 million years (becoming extinct within the last 40,000 years). At times, these and other predecessor species coexisted. Currently, *Homo sapiens* is the only surviving hominid species. See *Human Origins: What Bones and Genomes Tell Us About Ourselves,* by Rob DeSalle and Ian Tattersall. DeSalle and Tattersall are specialists and curators at the American Museum of Natural History in New York City. See www.amnh.org/exhibitions/permanent/humanorigins/.

For a more nuanced and extensive look, including the remarkable Neanderthals and Cro-Magnons, see Jared Diamond's *Guns, Germs, and Steel: The Fate of Human Societies,* 35–52. Also, see Ann Gibbons's *The First Human: The Race to Discover Our Earliest Ancestors* for a look at the history of the search for our predecessor species. And see Chris Stringer and Peter Andrew's *The Complete World of Human Evolution.*

the fittest."[13] Everything is relational in God's world. To be out of relationship, to go it alone, is lethal.

For 200,000 years, this evolving species of *Homo sapiens* lived amid the community of life in God's garden. First emerging in central Africa, our ancestors migrated in periodic waves far and wide throughout that African continent (150,000 years ago), into the Fertile Crescent and southern Asia (80,000 years ago), into southern Europe and the Iberian Peninsula (60,000, 40,000, and 10,000 years ago), into Australasia and the Oceania Islands (65,000, 30,000, and 10,000 years ago), into China (40,000 years ago), and into North and South America (perhaps as early as 25,000 years ago). These migrations were prompted by factors such as climate volatility, the advancing and receding of Ice Age sheets, animal and hunting routes, food requirements, exploration, and natural wandering. Further, the waves were not one way, but were back and forth over and over again.[14]

Earth became populated with thousands and thousands of clans and tribes and cultures that spread over time around the planet. Some of these developed into recent manifestations, which I have located in geographical regions currently named as follows: the Akoa of Africa, Bushmen of the Kalahari, Onabasula of New Guinea, Ainu of the northern Japanese island of Hokkaido, Ninivak and Netsilik of Alaska, Walbiri of Australia's Northern Territory, Sikai forest nomads on the Malaysian-

---

13.   Charles Darwin (1809–1882) did not use the phrase "survival of the fittest" in his 1859 *The Origin of the Species*. An English contemporary, Herbert Spencer (1820–1903), coined that phrase and transferred it into the realm of human economic and military "struggle for existence." This became known as social Darwinism. See Francisco J. Ayala, *Darwin's Gift to Science and Religion*, 46.

14.   Scientists track *Homo sapiens* migration by examining bone fossils, gene pool markers (mitochondrial genome for females, Y chromosomes for males), archeological evidence, sedimentary deposit layers, linguistic/language analysis, tool comparisons, the spread of human carrying viruses like *hepatitis 6*, bacterium pathogens like *helicobacter pylori* (common in stomach ulcers), and even lice. See especially chapters 6 and 9 of Rob DeSalle and Ian Tattersall's *Human Origin: What Bones and Genomes Tell Us About Ourselves*, and chapter 6 of Francisco J. Ayala's *Darwin's Gift to Science and Religion*. Also see Gary Stix, "Traces of a Distant Past," *Scientific American* (July 2008): 56–63.

Thai border, Tibetan herders of Chanthong Plateau, Apaches of Oklahoma, Lacandons of Mexico, Nama of Namibia, Macuna of Columbia, Kreen-Akrore of South America, Yanomami and Kraho and Waurá and Canela of Brazil, Jarawa of the Andaman Islands, Florida Seminoles, Quechuas of Peru, Eskimos of Greenland, Lapps of Norway, Hadzas of Tanzania, Kafirs of Pakistan, pastoral Todas of the Nilgiri Hills in India, Veddas of Ceylon, Bununs of Taiwan, Highlanders of New Guinea, Tohono O'odham and Hopi of southwestern United States.[15]

Now as it so happened, according to God's creative process, members of *Homo sapiens* were scouts of sorts, even pioneers. This was the first species whose members developed certain more sophisticated levels of self-awareness, intellect, memory, language, symbolism, and tool-making.[16] However, though trailblazers, presumably to be followed and even surpassed by other species on this evolving journey of life, these members of *Homo sapiens* were quite underdeveloped in many other arenas:

- They could not fly or live under the sea.

---

15. These are just a few examples of the thousands and thousands of diverse ancient and descendent indigenous cultures that have lived on this planet. These groupings of *Homo sapiens,* each unique and varied, have found ways to live and evolve among the community of life. For our purposes, many of these have been or are peoples who take what is truly needed and leave the rest. Daniel Quinn calls such Earth dwellers "Leavers."

16. Actually other creatures make and use tools, for example birds, chimpanzees, and otters. And mammals, including elephants, dolphins, and apes, have self-awareness, long memories, and profound social ties. An African gray parrot can be taught to name and identify colors, shapes, numbers, and moods. A bonobo ape can be taught to understand thousands of human spoken words, and can communicate across species to humans using several hundred keyboard symbols. What about humor? Watch a litter of puppies or family of sea otters "playing." Mindless instinct, or something more? What is "the horse whisperer" phenomenon? A New Caledonian crow can solve problems and make tools. Orangutans can understand and respond to another individual's perspective, make logical and thoughtful choices, problem solve, and show incipient moral awareness. There are countless examples. Have humans underestimated the extent of intelligence, awareness, memory, intentionality, language, humor, and problem solving in God's garden? See Virginia Morell, "Inside Animal Minds," *National Geographic*, (March 2008): 36–61.

- They were clumsy on their feet compared to a mountain goat or mule.

- They had terrible hand-eye coordination compared to that of a squirrel.

- They ranked in the middle in terms of speed; they were faster than cows and slower than pumas.

- They could not change color like a chameleon, fish, or tree toad.

- They could not store water like a desert tortoise, Saguaro cactus, or Bactrian camel (which can go up to ten months without drinking water).

Yet, like every other creature, their particular combinations of abilities and disabilities proved sufficient.

Two biblical metaphors are instructive as we think about the human creature. First, consider Genesis 2:7. The writer of this earlier text, which dates from around 900 BCE, depicts the members of *Homo sapiens*, represented by Adam, as composed of soil and dirt (in Hebrew, *adamah*). Humans, like all other creatures, are Earthlings (dirtlings). We come from the soil and were made alive as Yahweh "breathed into their nostrils the breath of life."[17]

Second, a scribe several hundred years later, around 500 BCE, writes a similar thing in Genesis 1:26–27, though using very curious language. This scribe writes, "And God said, 'Let *us* make human-

---

17. One should note the order that the writers of this earlier Genesis chapter 2 story suggest. They place the creation of a male member of *Homo sapiens* first, followed by that of plants (Genesis 2:4–5, 7–9), then animals (Genesis 2:18–19), and finally a female member of *Homo sapiens* as the culmination. This order is quite dissimilar to the later story in Genesis chapter 1, which places the creation of both female and male members of *Homo sapiens* at the end, after the plants and animals, and as God's final act on the sixth day.

     In the new framing presented in this book, not only do members of *Homo sapiens* emerge hundreds of millions of years into the story of life, but countless other species have come into existence since our arrival, and will continue to do so. It is thus incomplete to insist that humans are God's final and therefore paramount creature.

kind in *our* image'" (emphasis added). To whom is God talking? And who are "us" and "our"? The Trinity? A heavenly host of some kind? A royal "we"? Or could the storyteller be suggesting that humans are fashioned to mirror both the image of God *and* the image of the other evolving creatures in God's garden of life? In other words, when the Creator says, "Let us make humans in our image," God is talking to the fish and oceans, plants and animals, insects and forests of the garden. If so, it would seem predictable then that a self-understanding that exalts humanity above the rest of creation, which psychologically and theologically discon-nects (cuts off) our species from the wider community of life (our "family of origin" in family systems thinking) would not only be against God's intentions but also produce significant neurosis. Or as one farmer put it, "The farther humans get away from the dirt, the crazier they become!"

God loved Earth's garden. And though the garden could prosper nicely without *Homo sapiens* and wouldn't miss human-kind for a minute, God welcomed these creatures as much as the others, breathing into their very being the extraordinary dignity, meaning, and purpose given to all life forms.

As trailblazers, humans were charged with significant responsibility. They were charged, along with all other crea-tures, with the privilege and responsibility of caring for the garden during their stay. They would join the company of care-takers, along with God, of the evolving Tree of Life. The concepts of "tilling and keeping" (Genesis 2:15), "naming" (Genesis 2:19–20), and even "dominion" (Genesis 1:26–31) refer to God's intentions for humanity to be the pioneering, though not culmi-nating, species. It should be obvious that these concepts mean stewardship, and the healthy sharing of mutual relationship with other created things, like family members attending to one another, rather than reckless disregard or abuse. The notions of care and stewardship have been prominent in the teachings of *some* branches of Christianity for centuries, though in general not in Christianity's practice. In other words, there has been an inconsistency between orthodoxy (right thinking) and orthopraxis (right practice).[18]

Further, God reached out in relationship. This cannot be proven scientifically of course, but is a belief of many religions, including Christianity. God's involvement in garden life included more than establishing mechanical laws of nature. The Creator was concerned not just with functionality, but also well being, not just management, but care. The Creator wanted to know and be known in a relational covenant of love and trust, not just with humans, but with all creatures. We can observe one of the writers of the Noah parable saying as much: "Then God said to Noah and to his sons with him, 'As for me, I am establishing my covenant with you and your descendants after you, and with every living creature that is with you, the birds, the domestic animals, and every animal of the Earth with you, as many as came out of the ark'" (Genesis 9:8–10). In other words, creation is not an object to God, but a subject with whom to dance.

It should be noted that while strict evolutionary theory may require some kind of "creation myth" in order to explain origins—why anything exists at all, whether there ever was a time when there was nothing, how nothing came to be some-thing—nevertheless, this theory sees no necessity for a designer God to guide the process of evolving life once the process gets started. In fact, that is the point, making Darwin's contribution to human thinking somewhat counterintuitive. Darwin's unique inversion of reasoning points to a kind of bubble-up theory of

---

18.   If the biblical writers of Genesis 1:26 intended the word "dominion" to mean the objectification and subjugation of Creation, which always leads to misuse, then I disagree with them. However, there is another way to think of this. A parent has dominion in relation to a child. Here dominion means care and nurturance so that the child may grow up in health and well being. In marriage also, in a sense, a wife has dominion in relation to her husband, and a husband to his wife. This self-giving love is not meant to be domineering or manipulative, but allows the other to be protected and to flourish, so that the marriage relationship and all members of the family may thrive. It is never acceptable for "dominion" to mean exploitation or abuse. In my view, if this is what the biblical writers meant, which they *could* have, then I believe the word should be discarded as destructive and contrary to more principled notions of accountability and stewardship.

evolving life. Smaller and less intelligent forms of life don't require larger and more intelligent forms of life, like a creator God, to make them. The atom doesn't need a molecule, or the cell a larger organism. In Darwin's thinking, smaller and less intelligent/complex things come first. Then they sometimes evolve into larger and more intelligent/complex things. Certainly, God could exist, according to many evolutionary theorists. It's just that a divine designer God *per se* is not necessary for evolution to work. So it must be confessed that my belief in a Creator God who is involved in and interacts with the processes of smaller and less intelligent forms of life evolving into larger and more intelligent forms of life probably doesn't hold water for some scientists. That is, it is a tenet of my faith, not science.[19]

Following the pathway and the accumulated biological wisdom of 3.8 billion years of life on Planet Earth, including between 660 million to 1.2 billion years of multiple cell life, and 3 to 4 million years of predecessor species living and dying, *Homo sapiens* continued to evolve for nearly 200,000 years. Like their ancestors and all other creatures, they had the following characteristics:

- They drew wisdom from the lessons of garden life in order to survive.

- They trusted the Creator to rule the garden and provide what was truly needed.[20]

---

19.   Lucas John Mix points out that for life as we know it to exist and evolve (and to date, life on Earth is the only life we know), the medium of water, the basic material of carbon, and the energy of electrons and protons are all requisite. Yet it is still a mystery how life actually comes into being, that is, how chemistry (nonlife) evolves into biochemistry (beginning life) and eventually into biology and physiology. See *Life in Space: Astrobiology for Everyone*, especially chapters 3 and 6.

20.   This is a theological assertion, since anthropologists have to date only discovered specimens of artwork from 30,000 years ago that imply concepts of spirituality. My assertion stems from my belief that the Creator has always been in relationship with creation.

- They cherished life without hoarding it.[21]

- They lived and worked according to God's laws of nature.[22]

- They took what was required and left the rest.[23]

Because every species, including humankind, kept its hands off the Tree of the Knowledge of Good and Evil, created life flourished for eons and eras. It evolved under God's capable rule. If certain species emerged that were unable to live according to God's way, they soon detached from the Tree of Life and became extinct. This, too, was ultimately for the good of all.

The Tree of Life had many features. There was freedom of living. There was sufficiency and sustainability. There was great diversity. A Himalayan yak had to live differently than a Costa Rican iguana. An African termite couldn't expect to survive using a Beluga whale's life skills. Gila woodpeckers and mariposa lilies had different needs from those of the species *Homo sapiens,* Pacific Leatherback sea turtles, or 1,500-year old Bristlecone pine trees. And unlike the evolving mammals, which gave live birth to fully formed babies, marsupials such as the kangaroo delivered bean-sized offspring that then crawled into the mother's pouch for two months of nursing and safety before

---

21. The important distinction between cherishing and hoarding will be discussed later.

22. God's laws of nature include the laws of gravity and aerodynamics, electromagnetism, strong nuclear force and weak nuclear force, and biology and genetics. They include patterns of living that sustain life, including the food chain, limited competition as opposed to totalitarian annihilation, natural cycles of life and death, horticulture as opposed to totalitarian agriculture, emotional fields, triangles, balance, and diversity. They include all things the Creator has incorporated into the cosmos to sustain and further the evolving Tree of Life.

23. Daniel Quinn refers to these indigenous peoples as "Leavers," as opposed to "Takers." Leavers, those who learn from the community of life to take what they need and leave the rest, have managed to survive and thrive in God's garden for generations and generations. Will it be the same for Takers?

tackling the outside world.[24]

Further, there were thousands of right ways to be human. As my anthropologist friend Dianna Repp puts it, "Pastoralists in the East African savannah by necessity lived differently from those living in the highlands of South America. People in the Arctic north required different skill sets than those living in the humid tropical regions that belt the Earth. Even groups in close proximity developed unique social structures and gender roles that suited their needs as they perceived them." Most wouldn't have thought of imposing their way of life on others. There have always been and will always be different ways to be human residents on this Earth.

It's important not to idealize or downgrade garden life for any of God's creatures. Garden life was and never will be entirely blissful or entirely wretched. It was neither paradise nor hellish, perfect nor desolate. Rather, it was alive. Earthquakes, thunderstorms, bacteria, forest fires, and hurricanes have been there from the beginning and all enact their God-given purpose. In the aliveness of God's garden, there was and is struggle and joy, tragedy and triumph, and everything in between. This is life. This is the gift that has been evolving for eons. But even in times of individual heartbreak or grand disaster, the Creator has sewn succor, sustenance, and resilience into the very fabric of garden living. Managing the world is extremely complex and nuanced, but God does it well for the ongoing and evolving sake of all, and

---

24. This diversity cannot be overstated. Even modes of transport are incredibly varied, including slinking, sliding, burrowing, hitching a ride, creeping, crawling, walking, darting, galloping, leaping, flapping wings, beating wings, soaring, hovering, swimming, paddling, launching, floating, or jetting through water. Feeding techniques include the grippers, grabbers, spearers, drillers (Af deer fly), snatchers, choppers, crushers, munchers, or cutters. Some critters swallow whole; others suck through long tongues (sphinx moth). Some filter (minke whale), while others shoot lethal juices. A single square foot of soil is the fertile residence of millions of species, including decomposers like microbes, rove beetles, and fungal hyphae; grazers like springtails, nematode worms, and oribotid mites; and miniature predators like mites, hunting rove beetles, and pseudo scorpions. (My thanks to the Field Museum of Natural History in Chicago for the information in this footnote.)

for God's wider purposes in creating the creation at all.[25]

Neither should one romanticize or demonize *Homo sapiens*. As a species, early humans were neither ideal nor inferior, neither angels nor devils, neither overly wise nor overly stupid—and neither are modern humans. Nor were they noble savages. Rather, they were alive. There were even skirmishes on the borders between cultures as competing groups with their different interests rubbed up against each other. This is natural for any species trying to share space and resources. But according to God's way and the way of life within the garden, atypical was the culture that sought to exterminate the other either by totalitarian warfare, ecological destruction, food and species demolition, or ruthless imperialism (that is, economic, political, religious, or linguistic conquest).

As with all other creatures in the garden, humans then and now experienced life and death. And though life is to be cherished, it is not to be hoarded. The difference between the cherishing and hoarding of life is an important distinction to consider. For some, dying may come at birth. For others, it may come later in life, from a hurricane or disease or failed organ or simply old age. Not only does life produce both life and death, but the decomposed materials of death also produce life. Beginnings and endings and endings and beginnings are the way of God's garden, for the sake of the ongoing, evolving community of life. Because the cessation of life is as natural and inevitable as the beginning of life, to cherish it is a gesture of acknowledgement and respect; but to hoard it entails a deep misunderstanding.

The Creator intended members of *Homo sapiens* to live close to the Earth as part of a grand biodiversity of ever-evolving webs of sustainability. Or as the prophet Isaiah described, "They shall build their houses and inhabit them; they shall plant vineyards

---

25. Christian theology has occasionally pondered God's motivation for being "the maker of heaven and Earth." Is it for fulfillment? Entertainment? Relationship? Most renderings restrict the dynamic of God's relationship to humans. The framing of this book argues that such interpretation is overly anthropocentric (*Homo sapiens* centered), setting up the set of circumstances of destruction that part II addresses.

and eat their fruit. They shall not build and another inhabit; they shall not plant and another eat. For like the days of a tree shall the days of my people be, and my chosen shall long enjoy the work of their hands. They shall not labor in vain, or bear children for calamity" (Isaiah 65:21–23a).

By the way, God thought that this garden of life, with all its past, current, and yet to be diversity of being and ways of living, was good, *tov* in Hebrew. Very *tov* (Genesis 1:31)!

Part I poses the question, What if Christians were to embrace the notion of an evolving creation, recognizing that this evolution has been taking place over billions of years? Such a scenario opens up all kinds of interesting questions. How has God related to the community of life during these eons? How has the Creator interacted with *Homo sapiens* and our predecessor species for the 3 to 4 million years prior to our current era? And why, after all those years of hominid living, including 200,000 years of *Homo sapiens* living and 70,000 years of modern *Homo sapiens* living, did the religious belief systems of Judaism and Christianity only emerge a mere 4,000 and 2,000 years ago, respectively? Why so late in the game? What precipitated God to take such actions? Why was it directed at humans? And why was the main message of both Judaism and Jesus of Nazareth the announcement of the "reign of God"? Had humans become the one species that forgot whose world this is?

Further, part I proposes that the guiding principle of evolution is not so much "survival of the fittest" as it is survival of those species that "fit in," that is, that live within the conditions and parameters established by God to make flourishing life possible and sustainable. Those conditions are transcribed into the laws of nature for the good of all. For humans, and I would argue for other species now and in the future, those conditions have a conscious relational dimension. That is, we are granted the sacred privilege of being in a mindful relationship with the Creator. We are assigned the noble duty of helping to see that the Tree of all Life continues to evolve and flourish, or at least is not hindered. To fail in this trust is to fail as a species.[26]

So what has gone wrong? How did this one species among millions grow to be such a danger? To begin to answer this, we turn to the biblical/theological event/concept known as the Fall.

---

26. While I want to strongly affirm a "stewardship" role for humanity in the care of creation, that doesn't mean God's garden needs humans in order to survive or thrive, or that it's all about us. In fact, the community of life has done quite well without *Homo sapiens* for 99 percent of its history. It has flourished, adapted, and continued evolving. The overall ecosystem has not been seriously threatened until now.

Having said this, we must also acknowledge that while the curve of life's diversity has climbed through time, there have also been periodic mass extinctions. These include sweeping extinctions 465 million years ago (MYA), 370 MYA, 251 MYA, 225 MYA, and most recently, 65 MYA. During this last occurrence, dinosaurs and half of all known species disappeared. Theories for this sudden event include some combination of 1) the effects of a 10 km Chicxulub meteorite crashing along Mexico's Yucatan peninsula with an impact of 10^{14} tons of TNT, which caused massive Earthquakes and sent clouds of debris into the skies, blocking sunlight, rearranging the biosphere, and wiping out food systems; 2) an increase in volcanic activity, which released new and dangerous toxins into the atmosphere; and 3) continental drift, which, along with lowered water levels, enabled diseases to migrate between continents (at the beginning of the dinosaur period there was one basic continent, Pangaea, which began splitting up 200 million years ago).

Part Two
The Fall: A Tragedy Come Late

Chapter 4
Mutiny

In the Christian story, a theological concept/event known as the Fall plays a pivotal role in the history of the created world (as related in Genesis 3). Its implications reverberate throughout the entire Hebrew and Christian scriptures.

Curiously, neither the Apostles' nor the Nicene creeds mention this episode. Both historic statements of the Christian faith transition in one jarring leap from the creation of the universe to the birth of Jesus. This is a little like omitting the iceberg from the sinking of the Titanic![27]

But the Fall—its occurrence, meaning, aftermath, and God's

---

27. Then again, the historic ecumenical creeds don't mention the life and ministry of Jesus of Nazareth either. They move immediately from "born of the virgin Mary" to "suffered under Pontius Pilate, was crucified, died, and was buried." What happened in the meantime? What about the healings, teachings, conflicts with powers and principalities, temptations, actions of faithfulness, rejection by friends, and message? Perhaps it is time to rewrite the Christian creeds.

response—is central to the Christian narrative.[28]

Usually the concept/event, at least in traditional Roman Catholic and Western Protestant Christianity, is described this way: among the trees of the Garden of Eden, God put one tree in the middle of the region and declared it off limits to all creatures, including humans. This tree was called the Tree of the Knowledge of Good and Evil (Genesis 2:9). No one knows why. With the prohibition came a dire warning: "In the day that you eat of it you shall die." Well, Eve and Adam together ate. At that point, so the theology goes, sin and death infiltrated the species *Homo sapiens*. From that day onward, a human child birthed by a couple on the Iberian Peninsula, or the Nile River delta, or the plains of South Dakota was inevitably born sinful by nature. There was no escape. All of humanity was lost.

In addition, according to this traditional view, creation itself became broken, producing for the first time hurricanes, disease, droughts, bacteria, death and other non-Utopian imperfections. The Garden of Eden had been seen as paradise, with no death. Now all of creation, including humanity, was infected by this Original Sin of the first humans, with the sting of death being the ultimate effect.[29]

This is a widely recognized version of the story. Another

---

28. In describing this narrative, I have decided not to use the term "Judeo-Christian," a coupling generally unacceptable to Jews. Jewish believers no more grant that Christianity flowed from their religion than do Christians grant that Islam or Mormonism flowed from theirs. The term "Judeo-Christian" has a supersessionist, even imperialistic, tone.

29. It is interesting that Original Sin is stressed neither in Judaism nor in Eastern Orthodox Christianity. Judaism stresses more the rainbow promise at the end of the Noah story as a sign of full restoration from the effects of Adam and Eve's sin. "The Lord said, 'I set my bow in the cloud, and it shall be a sign of the covenant between me and the Earth'" (Genesis 9:13).

Eastern Orthodox Christianity also stresses more the notion of Original Blessing, which says that while sin certainly exists and needs to be dealt with, creation and humanity are fundamentally good. See Matthew Fox, *Original Blessing*. This is true of much of African spirituality as well. It is Western Christianity that has strained over Original Sin.

version, more common to my Lutheran tradition (I'm part of the Evangelical Lutheran Church in America, or ELCA), understands that Adam and Eve were not historical persons. Rather, they are metaphors for our humanity. While saying this may shock some people, among biblical scholars and theologians and bishops and pastors of the ELCA and many other Christian communities (including United Methodist, Presbyterian, American Baptist, Episcopalian, United Church of Christ, and even some Roman Catholic), this is an almost universal understanding. Adam and Eve were not actual persons. Actually, to cast them as the *bona fide* and unbirthed first parents (did they have belly buttons?) who populated the Earth by having sexual intercourse with each other and producing children, who in turn had sexual intercourse with their siblings and cousins and uncles and aunts and in-laws and so on, is at least morally problematic, if not scientifically and theologically far-fetched.

As a parable, then, in this interpretation, the characters of Adam and Eve symbolically represent the nature of our fundamental problem as human beings, which is that *we want to be (like) God*. Genesis 3:4–7 describes it this way as the crafty one said to Eve,

> "You will not die, for God knows that when you eat of it your eyes will be opened, and *you will be like God* [emphasis added], knowing good and evil." So when Eve saw that the tree was good for food, and that it was a delight to the eyes, and that the tree was to be desired to make one wise, she took of its fruit and ate; and she also gave some to her husband who was with her, and he ate. Then their eyes were opened, and they were exposed.[30]

Such strutting hubris and the harmful effects that steamroll through history have now gone on for so long that all human-

---

30. Again, I will at times cite passages from the Hebrew and Christian scriptures. These quotes are meant to be references in the story rather than "proof-texts" to prove my point. Regarding biblical interpretation see appendix A, *Biblical Interpretation*.

kind has become inextricably entangled in a web of sin and brokenness. Daniel Erlander describes this sin aptly in his book *Manna and Mercy*:

> Humans decided to find joy by becoming BIG DEALS (Gen. 3:1–7). How did humans know if they were big deals? They knew by bossing other humans around, by piling up stuff, by dominating nature, and by reaching glorious heights of health and beauty and knowledge. They also knew by having more points than other humans in their scoring systems.
>
> Humans gathered into groups, clans, tribes, and nations. These collections of humans became extremely enthused about their group being better than other groups. Thus humans invented oppression and war. Oppression involves setting up a system so one group can use another group for its own advantage. War involves killing humans in another group until they surrender. War provides an obvious way to know which group is best. The winners are always the biggest deals. [31]

We should note that this is not how the Creator behaves, but rather how a creature behaves when it thinks it is God. This would also come to be known as Original Sin, and would be understood by the apostle Paul as applying to all of humanity, "For there is no distinction, since all have sinned and fall short of the glory of God" (Romans 3:22b–23).

---

31. Daniel Erlander, *Manna and Mercy*, 2. Erlander insightfully describes the sinful tendency to develop point systems that allow us to measure one another's value and render ourselves superior.

These are common understandings of the Fall within historic Christianity. But might we consider a new scenario? The following is an attempt to do just that. It differs quite strikingly from traditional and even nontraditional ideas. It is a startling reconsideration, one that I had never examined, let alone heard, until reading the works of Daniel Quinn. (Several of Quinn's books are listed in the bibliography and more can be found at www.ishmael.org.) Doing so has changed my world-view and is transforming the way I live my life. It has provided for me a more feasible design for understanding Earth's history, Christian theology, and the daily task and privilege of living.

Quinn proposes that the stories of Adam and Eve were not meant to describe single, actual persons who once lived, who through their disobedience somehow triggered the lethal infection of all subsequent humanity, and even Earth life itself. In this way, his view is dissimilar to the first interpretation of the Genesis stories mentioned earlier, one held by many people of various Christian traditions. But according to Quinn, and this is equally significant, neither are Adam and Eve primarily symbolic. They are also not meant to serve as metaphors for what is timelessly considered by the storytellers to be amiss in human nature. They are not, for example, meant to represent us modern folks who through our thinking and behaviors disobey God's commands, try to play the role of God, deflect responsibility, blame others, and so on. While we certainly do these things, this is not what the Adam and Eve stories were about. Rather—and this is Quinn's intriguing insight—these stories were meant primarily to be specific to the time and locale of the storytellers. They were attempts by the writers to understand and articulate actual and troubling historical changes in actual historical times that the storyteller's community was experiencing. In other words, the authors created parables to describe worrisome shifts in garden living that they were witnessing in their corner of the world during their generation.

Following this line of reasoning, an additional concept emerges, namely that what Genesis describes as the Fall is in fact a relatively *recent* occurrence. This is significant. In the long evolutionary history of life on Planet Earth (over 3.7 billion years), and the briefer evolutionary history of the species *Homo sapiens* (over 200,000 years), the Fall story refers to changes occurring not long ago. It refers to troubling ways of living and thinking that were beginning to occur among isolated portions of the human community a mere 6,000 to 10,000 years prior to today—a blink of an eye really—according to Quinn. These troubling ways had gained traction and were spreading. They were seeping into heretofore unaffected regions. And they were now being witnessed and experienced by the biblical story-tellers several thousand years later in their own specific time and locale. In other words, these storytellers were composing parables to describe unsettling changes in thinking, worldview, self-understanding, and behavior that were actually infiltrating their community from someplace else.

Such an understanding has profound implications for the story of human life. What follows is an attempt to address those implications. It is an attempt to configure an alternative version of Earth's story, humanity's story, and God's story, and especially how human history has arrived at the place of peril it finds itself today.

Chapter 5
Menace

From the beginning, God's creative process embarked on a journey of diversity, balance, and rigor. With God as presiding minister, the garden burst forth with green scenes of towering trees; rippled streams flowing with insects and fish; mountain peaks grinning fall-colored reflections on mirrored lakes; tenacious snow patches blanketing giant boulders; berries and wild greens; heavy rains dimpling deep-forest backwaters; and the wonderful sounds of squawking, chittering, chattering, growling, prattling, garish, and noisy life. God was indeed making a stunning habitation!

Homo sapiens, too, lived for generations upon generations in God's garden. Within God's garden there arose numerous ways for humans to live, including a variety of valid economic and political systems, religious and philosophical creeds, sexual roles and gender identities, and family structures. The way of life for one culture may have involved hunting and fishing, and for another gathering edible gourds and wild berries. Certain environments coaxed some people to plant vegetables and hunt large game and erect buildings, and others to harvest wild grains and domesticate animals like llamas, cows, and chickens. Some utilized materials such as wood, stone, bone, antlers, and shells, while others focused on ivory, hides, and copper. Plant materials were used for weaving baskets, cords, and rope for some, and sandals, nets, and clothing for others. Some learned to use medicinal plants such as tea (stomach ailments), poultices (sprains and swellings), powders and soaps (antiseptic washes), and fumigants. Certain boats seem to have come on the scene some 40,000 years ago, assisting migrants to Australia. There is evidence of other watercraft (such as the predecessors of the Eskimo kayak, Algonquian birch bark canoe, Nootka dugout, and Chumash plank boat) appearing in other parts of the world about 13,000 years ago. Nomadic peoples lived in the lowlands during winter and in the upper altitudes through summer. Most cultures leaned toward patriarchal expressions of authority and lineage, but others (such as the Hopi, Iroquois, and Huron) leaned toward the matriarchal.

Further, a home might have taken the form of a lean-to, plank house, long house, Earth lodge, or hogan for some, and a tepee, wigwam, igloo, pit house, or pueblo for others. Various cultures depended more on pottery, shell work, baskets, beads, and feather work, while others developed useful forms of painting, dyeing, engraving, stonework, woodwork, and skin-work. And while the indigenous peoples of Baffin Island in the Arctic Archipelago wore layers and layers of clothing, it would have been foolish for the inhabitants of Fiji or the Kalahari to wear any clothing at all. What was normative for one grouping of *Homo sapiens* depended on how well their way of life complemented God's garden in their locale. If it didn't, they soon moved on or died out, just as God's laws of nature were designed to affect all species.[32]

But then something happened, something evil. This is Quinn's insight, which I find particularly intriguing.

This evil had to do with a huge change in thinking, a substantial shift in self-understanding, a titanic revision of worldview. It happened among one species in God's garden, namely *Homo sapiens*. Actually, the change in thinking didn't occur in all members of *Homo sapiens,* only in a portion. And what began with great promise in their minds soon devolved into terror. This was the Fall.

Evil was a relatively new thing to the community of life and should not to be confused with other necessary and natural activities that made the garden alive, namely birth, death, Earthquakes (tectonic plate subduction recycles geological materials

---

32. It's striking to consider the variety and quantity of peoples who have populated the Earth. In western British Columbia's Georgia Strait region alone, numerous tribes have lived for thousands of years. Today's manifestations of some of those First Nation groupings include the Holmaco, Klahoose, Sliammon, Comox, Qualicum, SeShalt, Sne-Nay-Mux, Squamish, Quwutsun, Stoilo, Semiahanoo, Tslei-waututh, Musqueam, Tsawwassen, Esquimult, Songhees, Saanich, Coquitlam, each with distinct ways of living and being.

    Similarly, in what is currently Arizona, there are the Navajo, Hopi, Yuma, Hualapai, Havasupai, Shivwits, Yuma, Cocopah, Pima, Tohono O'odham, Akimel O'odham, Maricopa, Chemehueri, Quechan, Kamia, Yavapai, Walapai, Chiricahua Apache, and Pasqua Yaqui cultures and peoples. See the books *Paths of Life: American Indians of the Southwest and Northern Mexico*, edited by Thomas E. Sheridan and Nancy J. Parezo, and *Atlas of the North American Indian*, by Carl Waldman, to get a sense of the vast assortment of cultures in God's garden.

from inside the planet up to the surface and down again),[33] rain, thunder, lightning, wind, volcanic activity (Earth's internal heat machine keeps the planet "alive"), seasonal change, hurricanes (how else to scatter the accumulated heat around the equator belt to other parts of the globe?),[34] bacteria, viruses, sexuality, termites, sunsets, tides (thought to have sparked the movement of sea life unto land, and some land life back into the sea),[35] drought, floods (to replenish the soil), forest fires (to regenerate

---

33. Continents are now understood to be not permanent land masses surrounded by water, but rather giant rafts floating on molten rock. At one time contiguous, these colossal, moving (as much as four inches per year) tracts of land have in the past 200 million years shifted apart. Such continental drift explains both Earthquakes and why oddly similar species such as the emu of Australia, the ostrich of Africa, and the rheas of South America exist on continents currently separate by thousands of miles of ocean.

34. It is true that current destructive conditions relating to climate change likely are connected to human malfeasance. These behaviors appear to have exacerbated natural occurrences such as forest fires and hurricanes. However, this doesn't diminish the fact that forest fires and hurricanes are integral to the way God made the world. They have important purposes for the evolving Tree of Life.

    This of course brings up sticky questions relating to "theodicy" and "God's will." Was it God's will, for example, that Hurricane Katrina struck New Orleans and the surrounding Gulf Coast in 2005? This disaster brought great suffering to many creatures, including humans. Did God want this to happen? This is a tough question. My own response is yes and no. I don't believe God uses what we call "natural disasters" to "send messages" or to enact blessings or curses upon the community of life. In that sense, God did not cause Hurricane Katrina. However, in another sense the Creator did cause it, because such phenomena are built into the necessary workings of the evolving Tree of Life. This is a difficult concept, and for some it may cause them to want to distance themselves from the Creator. For me, it makes me more curious and draws me closer. In parts IV and V, I intend to explore (though not solve) this conundrum.

35. All sea mammals evolved *from* the land. Some 50 million years ago certain land mammals living at the water's edge began returning to the sea for good, becoming fully aquatic over a 10-million-year span. Whales and dolphins share genetic relatedness with hippopotamuses, pigs, camels, antelope, and cattle. Manatees and dugongs are related to elephants. Seals, sea lions, and walruses share DNA with bears and dogs. And sea otters appear to have evolved from weasels. All sea mammals need to come to the surface to breathe air into their lungs, though some whale species can hold their breath for up to one hour.

vegetation and clean out excess insect populations), snowfalls, joy, sorrow, youth, middle age, old age, love, fear, anger (some experiences should make us angry), and trust.

This new phenomenon called evil should also not be confused with certain other irksome behaviors that naturally occur among many species, including humans. These include jealousy, gossip, misplaced lust, theft, lying, greed, and even murder. Granted, these can and do escalate into situations of great trouble. And certainly minimizing behaviors based on these and replacing them with healthier expressions will lead to greater quality of living for all. But in this new framing, these "sins" weren't really the main problem. The new thing was something infinitely more perverse. It was rebellion. It was insurgence against God. It was disregard for the laws of nature and the ethical design inherent in God's community of life since its foundation.

Here is how the evil thing happened:

Not long ago, about 6,000 to 10,000 years ago,[36] one or more particular groups or cultures of *Homo sapiens* residing in one or more particular locales of the garden, perhaps an area such as the Fertile Crescent or western China, came up with a startling notion. This notion was new upon the face of the Earth, or at least had never taken root. The new notion was that *Homo sapiens* were special. They also came to believe that the laws of God's rule implanted in the community of life since the begin-

---

36. Daniel Quinn suggests these dates. They coincide with a change well into the discovery and implementation of crop growing, including the use of various irrigation systems and seed storage, when agriculture gradually turned totalitarian. The dates and locations cannot be pinpointed. What is clear, however, is that a sea change took place in worldview and behavior among some *Homo sapiens*. What can be documented as the norm before became something else after. What this something else is will become clearer with further reading.

ning DID NOT APPLY to humans. That is, humans were exempt. This notion didn't occur in one person or at one moment, or even in the course of several centuries, but emerged over many, many generations.

Following this line of thinking, the members of these very few cultures surmised the following:

- Humans were exceptional.

- Humans were meant to be distinct from the community of life.

- Humans were meant to be superior to the community of life.

- Human life was at odds with all other life forms.

Such thinking was unprecedented among God's creatures, and until then unheard of among members of *Homo sapiens*. Further, they concluded the following:

- God's garden was created primarily for the sake of humans.

- Humans were free to do with it what they pleased.

- God's garden was to be regarded as valuable in proportion to its value for humans, or as the Greek philosopher Protagoras announced in the fifth century BCE, "Man is the measure of all things."[37]

The Fall involved even more. These particular cultures also began to treat the garden as if it were a jungle, that is, a dangerous, deficient, defiant, disorderly *enemy*. They came to believe that the garden was wild and needed to be tamed,

---

37. The seventeenth century philosopher Francis Bacon (1561–1626) presumed a similar view of superiority, claiming, "Man, if we look to final causes, may be regarded as the center of the world, insomuch that if man were taken away from the world, the rest would seem to be all astray, without aim or purpose." See Benjamin Kline, *First Alone the River*, 9.

was broken and needed to be fixed, was inept at self-rule and needed to be conquered, was a wasteland and needed to be "developed." All of this required the domination and rulership of *Homo sapiens*, they believed. They proclaimed this as not only holy destiny—that is, the Creator's intended way for humans to realize their fullest humanity—but also the way for the garden to fulfill its sacred purpose. In other words, humans were lords of the garden and should act as lords of the garden, and the garden should and would submit.

Breaching God's domain and crossing the line of differentiation between Creator and creature, these branches or groups belonging to *Homo sapiens,* emerging from one or several cultures in one or several locales in the world, began to infiltrate God's province. Ignoring the "no trespassing" sign, they ate of the fruit of the forbidden Tree of the Knowledge of Good and Evil. That is, they assumed God's ownership and governance. In doing so, they stepped in (fell) over their heads.

Now newly smart, although not wise (since humans can only eat of the fruit but cannot digest it), this one or more (not all) grouping(s) of *Homo sapiens* declared war on God's rule. They engaged in mutiny. No longer wanting to live at the hand of God as humans had done for ages, they began to take charge of life on Earth. Seduced by what they saw as their successes, they became enticed by the circumstantial evidence that they could run things better than God could.

They also declared war on the garden. As such, they began to live out a story/narrative that positioned *Homo sapiens* not only as the crown, the pinnacle, and the end (final goal) of the creative process, but also the garden's ultimate reason for existence. Accompanying this towering self-regard came not only a cynical devaluation of the intrinsic ways of God's garden, but also a marginalization of the acknowledgement of the reign of God.

They discarded horticulture and sustainable agriculture (living together with creation) and began practicing a strange kind of warfare called totalitarian agriculture (over against

Creation). They became insatiable consumers, multipliers, and conquerors. The term "totalitarian agriculture" is Daniel Quinn's term. It refers to what happens when a hundred-acre plot of land that has served as biomass and habitat for a variety of living creatures is scraped away and turned into mono-crop farm acreage or malls for humans. Certainly humans, like any creature, are entitled to their fair shares of food and space. And certainly food chains and food cycles are very much necessary to the inner workings of God's garden. The Creator has provided richly for the community of life with the principle that all have enough and no one has too much. But only this new culture of some *Homo sapiens* became addicted to the need for more and more, with little regard for what is trodden upon or pushed to extinction.[38]

They became Takers. The term "Taker" is also Daniel Quinn's term, and it contrasts another of his terms, "Leavers." Leaver peoples, in ancient times and currently, take what is needed and leave the rest. They see their lives as interwoven with the lives of all other creatures, as well as the soil, sea, and sky. They cherish and find security in their status as members of the whole community of life.

In contrast, Taker peoples take beyond what they need, and keep taking until they overrun other life forms. They consider this their right. They confer on themselves a status separate from, superior to, and the reason for the rest of creation. Rather than making their livings as though the world belongs to God and all God's creatures, Taker peoples make their living as though the world belongs to their species alone.

At one point, this Taker culture began killing for more than food, a behavior rarely seen among the creatures of God's garden. They killed out of greed. They killed out of hate. They killed out of lust for dominion.

---

38. I will use the word "totalitarian" to refer to this voracious individual or systemic appetite for more and more, especially when it is combined with a near total ignorance of, or willful disregard for, the communal (affecting the whole community of life) and long-term consequences.

And these Takers began to hoard and amass for themselves the bounty and the scarcity of God's manna in the garden. A portion of Israel's exodus story located in Exodus chapter 16 describes one such example of hoarding. In this episode, what is hoarded rots. It becomes foul-smelling. The moral? Hoarding stinks! The apostle Paul picked up this same ethical message in 2 Corinthians 8:15, referring to God's way as that in which "the one who had much did not have too much, and the one who had little did not have too little." In other words, all had enough and no one had too much. Daniel Erlander builds on this theme throughout his wonderful book *Manna and Mercy,* arguing that this fundamental value corresponds to faithful and sustainable human living. Noticeably, this value is ignored by almost all Christians in economically wealthy countries around the globe.

As the cancer spread, these wayward cultures also began locking up food. No other *Homo sapiens* society or tribe in history, and no other creature in God's garden, had ever put food under lock and key. Once food is incarcerated, people are forced to join Taker economic and political systems just to survive. Walter Brueggemann describes one tragic way the process unfolds in his article "The Liturgy of Abundance, the Myth of Scarcity: Consumerism and Religious Life." He describes how the mud pits of Pharaoh's Egypt became a showcase for a system where the food supply was controlled, administered, and monopolized. He writes:

> Genesis 47 . . . marks the first time in the Bible, someone says, "There's not enough. Let's get everything." Pharaoh hires Joseph to manage the monopoly. When the crops fail and the peasants run out of food, they come to Joseph. And on behalf of Pharaoh, Joseph says, "What's your collateral?" They give up their land for food, and then, the next year, they give up their cattle. By the third year of the famine they have no collateral but themselves. And that's how the children of Israel become slaves—through an economic transaction. By the end of Genesis 47 Pharaoh has all the land except that

belonging to the priests, which he never touches because he needs somebody to bless him.

In the modern world, educational systems, too, are forced to teach the Taker approach to life in order to be judged successful and cost-effective. And ironically, though all members of *Homo sapiens* have always had "organic" food, in our day such basic and ordinary fare has become a commercialized novelty accessible mostly to the very wealthy.

Such behavior was a stunning reversal within the Tree of Life, setting up members of *Homo sapiens* for regression as a species in wisdom and moral character, for the despoiling of God's creation, and for toil and discord. Strife is not a punishment or curse from God, but rather a predictable outcome that accompanies mutiny. As the writer of Genesis states, "Because you have listened to the voice of your wife, and have eaten of the tree about which I commanded you, 'you shall not eat of it,' cursed is the ground because of you; in toil you shall eat of it all the days of your life; thorns and thistles it shall bring forth for you; by the sweat of your face you shall eat bread, until you return to the ground, for out of it you were taken; you are dust, and to dust you shall return" (Genesis 3:17–19).

Today, scientists estimate that the biomass consumed by the world's 6.6 billion humans causes the extinction of over 30,000 species annually. This calculation is part of the permanent Evolving Planet exhibition at the Field Museum of Natural History in Chicago, as well as other references. That's more than eighty species destroyed forever during each twenty-four-hour period—by us. This kind of harm is part of a troubling legacy emanating from a series of historical events associated with the Fall. At the very least, the legacy poses questions of sustainability. It also poses questions of ethical integrity for Christians and others, especially since a small but significant portion of those 6.6 billion persons, that is, those of us in the United States and other rich nations, consume and pollute and destroy multiple times our share. And while it is true that high birthrates are a problem in some impoverished nations, it is also true that the average American family consumes, pollutes, and destroys eight times the world's average. Thus, a four-person household in the United States annually causes damage equivalent to a thirty-two-person community in an impoverished country. If the current population of the United States in the year 2010 is over 300 million, our nation's negative ecological impact is equivalent to a population of 2.4 billion.

Chapter 6
Losing Abel

It should be noted that in the Genesis story, God's ban regarding the Tree of the Knowledge of Good and Evil was not intended to *test* Adam and Eve. This ban was not an arbitrary exercise to see how far up or down the obedience scale humans might navigate. Rather, God's command was for the purpose of *protecting* the whole community of life, including humans. The Creator understood that no creature was capable of handling the power that the tree offered. Period. On the day a mere mortal/species tried to usurp God's governance, a culture of death was bound to commence. It would be like a two-year-old trying to fly a helicopter, a three-year-old performing laser eye surgery, or a mere politician or general being given the authority to launch weapons of mass destruction. They'd be in over their heads. Failure and tragedy would be the only monstrous and eventual outcomes.[39]

So storming God's province and staking claim to God's garden, this one branch (but not all) of *Homo sapiens* embarked on a culture-wide and eventually near species-wide campaign for dominion and domination. "Come, let us make a name for ourselves" was the way the writer of Genesis 11:4 expressed this new and pernicious worldview.

The storytellers of Genesis chapter 4 said it in another way. "Now Abel was a keeper of sheep, and Cain a tiller of the ground. In the course of time Cain brought to the LORD an offering of the fruit of the ground, and Abel for his part brought of the firstlings of his flock, their fat portions. And the LORD had regard for Abel and his offering, but for Cain and his offering he had no regard" (Genesis 4:2b–5a).

What was Cain's response to the Creator's preference for Abel? "Cain was very angry, and his countenance fell. The LORD said to Cain, 'Why are you angry, and why has your countenance fallen? If you do well, will you not be accepted? And if you do not do well, sin is lurking at the door; its desire is for you, but you must master it.' Cain said to his brother Abel, 'Let us go out to the field.' And when they were in the field, Cain rose up against his brother Abel, and killed him" (4:5b–7). Yes, Cain committed murder.

When God discerned the spilled blood of Abel crying from the soil and sought out Cain to determine what he might know about the situation, Cain responded to the questions "What have you done?" and "Where is your brother Abel?" (4:9–10) with a fearsome I-centeredness and a stunning disregard unheard of

---

39. Daniel Quinn notes how the traditional understanding of the story of the forbidden tree portrays a God who is morally problematic. Can you imagine a loving mother or father placing a loaded gun on the kitchen table and telling the children "don't touch" in order to test their obedience? What kind of parent is that? A disaster is waiting to happen. Surely God's ways are wiser. Quinn suggests a different interpretation. Rather than being a test, the biblical writers are portraying this ban as having a salvific purpose. It is a statement of God's reign. It is a declaration of God's ownership. It is an announcement that, "For the sake of life, stay away from messing with God's job!"

within the community of life, startling both the cosmos and Creator alike. Cain declared, "Am I my brother's keeper?" (4:9b).

Daniel Quinn, in his masterful novel *Ishmael*, makes a unique interpretation of this biblical story and equates "Taker" peoples with Cain and "Leaver" peoples with Abel. Cain represents those few cultures of *Homo sapiens* who in the storytellers' time were not only waging war against God's reign and against God's beloved garden, but were also waging war against the then vast majority of diverse *Homo sapiens* cultures and tribes and clans around the planet who were not joining Cain's mutiny. Quinn calls these favored ones who did not mutiny "Abel." What I find especially helpful about this view is that it provides a way of thinking about and exploring two distinct ways of living and being in this world. Abel represents those cultures that have lived *within* the community of life for ages and ages. Cain represents a more recent and aberrant culture(s) that sees *Homo sapiens* as separate from, superior to, in charge of, and the reason for the wider community of life.

Of the two, Abel cultures are preferred by the Creator. Below are some of the reasons:

- They keep their hands off of the Tree of the Knowledge of Good and Evil.

- They do not practice totalitarian agriculture.

- They do not carry out totalitarian consumerism.

- They forsake both hoarding and the locking up of food.

- Unlike the mutineers (Cain), they take what is needed and leave the rest, making their offerings *and* the means of their living pleasing to the Lord.

According to Quinn, while certainly exceptions can be found, these members of *Homo sapiens* who have lived the Leaver way of life are generally to be understood to be those people we consider "indigenous peoples."[40]

And just as it was in the days of old, so it is today; wherever Abel appears, Cain rises up to kill him.[41] Whenever Abel is "discovered," the powers and principalities of Cain's world inadvertently and advertently mobilize to engulf Abel's way of life. Where Cain cultures intersect with Abel cultures, Abel's land always manages to get seized, his natural resources commandeered, his means of living emasculated, his language destroyed, and the social order of his community trampled to the dust.

For 3 to 4 million years, and continuing even into the present, Abel's way of living has favorably complemented garden life. Had it not, *Homo sapiens* and their predecessor species would never have kept evolving. A species must live sustainably within the garden in order to keep evolving.

But Cain's culture now has gained the upper hand. In fact, Cain has become the dominant manifestation of our species. The record is startling. Spreading throughout every continent, Cain has dominated and overrun Abel time and crushing time

---

40. Some scholars question the phrase "indigenous peoples," because who got to a certain region first is always open to question. Humans roam. And there have been skirmishes fought over access to water, forests, and land. How far back does one go to determine first peoples? I'll be using the term "indigenous peoples" to refer to a worldview and way of life—a Leaver way of life. These peoples are not to be romanticized or demonized. However, generally, over generations and generations they have lived sustainably within the community of life. They rarely saw themselves as separate from or superior to other creatures, and it is still that way among tiny remnants of nearly disseminated Leaver cultures around the globe today. For example, when the Lakota peoples of South Dakota kill a doe for food, they do it with a profound (though, not sentimental) reverence for the sacrifice this "sister" is making for them. In other words, they see both the deer and themselves as members of the community of life.

It also makes sense then that the Genesis storytellers would have seen the cultures of Abel and Cain, though growing radically divergent in worldview and behavior, as siblings, as part of a common family. Hence, brothers are the characters in the story.

41. I'll be using male pronouns when referring to both Cain and Abel. However, it should be noted that men and women are often equal actors in this drama. And as with Adam and Eve, the Cain and Abel story is meant to refer to actual historical changes taking place.

again. Entire peoples have been decimated, whole cultures laid waste. Traditions have been lost, family systems broken up, and ecologies endangered to the brink of ruin. Like a cancer, Cain knows no boundaries and harbors no shame (see, for example, appendix B, *Cain Invades South America, 1532 CE,* for a firsthand account of the conquistadors from Spain as they crushed Inca families in South America).

Even in the United States, as in many Taker nations, Cain has been given medals of honor for exterminating Abel. Consider two "Indian fighter" generals, Andrew Jackson and William Henry Harrison. Not only did they receive accolades for their roles in genocide, they were also subsequently elected to the U.S. presidency. General Jackson became a national hero for killing native families. Later, as president (1829–1837), he ordered the relocation death marches of Cherokee peoples known as the "Trail of Tears," which took place in the 1830s. General William Henry Harrison also became a revered military leader for his role in the 1811 killing of Shawnee peoples at the junction of the Tippecanoe and Wabash Rivers in northern Indiana Territory. For this and other mass murders, he was given the nickname "Old Tip." His 1840 campaign slogan for the U.S. presidency, with running mate John Tyler, boasted "Tippecanoe and Tyler, too!" Packaged as a war hero, he won the election, though his death from pneumonia one month after Inauguration Day made Harrison our first president to expire while in office.

In executing this conquest upon the hundreds and hundreds of indigenous tribes and cultures in the Americas, Cain has waged "ideological as well as military and economic warfare against the integrity of Native culture."[42]

One could add human slavery to the list of tragic behaviors in many Taker nations. Ten U.S. presidents—George Washington, Thomas Jefferson, James Madison, James Monroe, Andrew Jackson, William Henry Harrison, John Tyler, James K. Polk, Zachary Taylor, and Andrew Johnson—men otherwise esteemed as intelligent, well-read, and morally upright, were also predators and perpetrators in the disturbing web of kidnappings, enslavement, cruelty, and murder in the buying, selling, and oppressing of African men, women, and children.[43]

When in February of 1861 Texas became the seventh state to formally vote to secede from the Union, and this during the interval between Abraham Lincoln's November election as president and his March 4 inauguration, the Texas convention declared,

> We hold as undeniable truths that the governments of the various States, and of the confederacy itself, were established exclusively by the white race. . . . That the African race had no agency in their establishment; that they were rightfully held and regarded as an inferior and dependent race. . . . That in this free government all white men are and

---

42. Carl Waldman, *Atlas of the North American Indian*, 228.

Some will insist that native families in the Americas died mostly from devastating epidemic diseases, especially smallpox, brought by Europeans. While it is true new diseases played a role, other health-diminishing factors such as enslavement, the systematic destruction of food sources, forced removal from ancestral lands, death marches, massacres, official lying, divide and conquer government policies, forced assimilation, broken treaties, and incessant domination were hardly incidental. To add insult to injury, when native peoples fought back to honorably defend their families and homeland, their actions, in the language of Cain-speak, were ironically associated with phrases such as "on the warpath," "Apache raid," "renegades," "hostile Indians," and "those savages."

43. Most American slaves were kidnapped from western African. Many came from communities and tribes such as the following: Wolof, Mandingo, Malinke, Bambara, Fulani, Papel, Limba, Bola, Balante, Tamne, Mende, Vai, De, Gola, Kisi, Hausa, Bassa, Brebo, Yoruba, Mupe, Fon, Ewe, Ga, Popo, Edo-Bini, Fante, Akan, Efik-Ibibio, Ijaw, Ibani, Igbos, Bakong, Malimbo, Bambo, Hdungo, Balimbe, Budongo, Luba, Loanga, and Ovimbundu.

of right out to be entitled to equal civil and political rights; that the servitude of the African race, as existing in these States, is mutually beneficial to both bond and free, and is abundantly authorized and justified by the experience of mankind, and the revealed will of the Almighty Creator, as recognized by all Christian nations."[44]

One wonders especially how followers of Jesus of Nazareth and Jesus the Christ became so distorted in their thinking and behavior.[45]

Curiously, Cain has been successful in creating a climate of exemption for participants in genocide, that is, generals, politicians, soldiers, judges, voters, etc., often insisting that they were just obeying orders; they were just enforcing the law; they were just furthering national security; or, ironically, fulfilling religious commandments from God. Perhaps this immunity could be examined more carefully. Perhaps affirming such reasoning not only strengthens Cain's Taker ways, but also dishonors Abel cultures and continues the destruction of God's garden.

Some may say, "We have no right to judge leaders and others of former times. We weren't there; it is not our place." This is part of the code of understanding of many of Cain's historians in academia, politics, and the press. It's interesting then that Cain's current leaders say, "Don't judge us now. Let history decide." Cain has learned much from the crafty one (Genesis 3:1).

---

44. William Lee Miller, *President Lincoln: The Duty of a Statesman*, 15.

45. Regarding slavery, it is true that Thomas Jefferson tried to insert the abolition of human slavery into the text of the Declaration of Independence in 1776. But his request was defeated. And it is true that George and Martha Washington, who together enslaved over 300 men, women, and children on their plantation at Mount Vernon, did make provisions in their will to grant freedom to those slaves once they had died. One wonders, however, why they didn't free them while they were still alive and could have assisted with the transition.

It is also true that among the hundreds of thousands of Abel-Leaver cultures found around the planet through the ages, one can find evidence of human slavery being practiced among a portion of them from time to time. Again, Abel is not to be romanticized. Nevertheless, it is Cain's cultures that have advanced this behavior to new levels of organization, the effects of which are still being felt in numerous cultures generations later.

As with the Fall story in Genesis chapter 3, Daniel Quinn also interprets the Cain and Abel story in Genesis chapter 4 as originally told by Abel storytellers from an Abel point of view. This Leaver community, which had lived adequately and sustainably for thousands of years, was experiencing confusion and frustration with their Taker neighbors to the north (or south or east or west) who were engaging in totalitarian agriculture/consumerism. They asked themselves: Why do these people behave this way? Why do they display such disregard for God's garden of life? Why do they overrun us with their Taker ways? They must think they are rulers of the world. They must have eaten from the Tree of the Knowledge of Good and Evil and consider themselves capable of such an undertaking. That's the only explanation. They are like this because they have mutinied against God and the community of life, and have become a culture at war.

And now, every creature of the garden, including Abel, fears the one whose forehead God has marked.[46]

After only 6,000 to 10,000 years, Cain's ways have spread far and wide. Consumed by a relentless quest of dominance, Cain has indeed become dominant and domineering. Conquistador, colonizer, imperialist, corporate devourer, totalitarian consumer, Cain knows only how to multiply, overrun, and destroy.

---

46. "Cain said to the Lord, 'My punishment is greater than I can bear! Today you have driven me away from the soil, and I shall be hidden from your face; I shall be a fugitive and a wanderer on the Earth, and anyone who meets me may kill me.' Then the Lord said to him, 'Not so. Whoever kills Cain will suffer a sevenfold vengeance.' And the Lord *put a mark on Cain*, so that no one who came upon him would kill him. Then Cain went away from the presence of the Lord, and settled in the land of Nod outside of the Garden" (Genesis 4:13–16, emphasis added). Notice that for the storyteller(s) capital punishment is not acceptable behavior for participants in the community of life, even if it is a response to Cain's culture of destruction.

One significant transformation in our species over the past 6,000 to 10,000 years has to do with population expansion. Our species is experiencing unsustainable growth. Could there be a connection between this fact and Cain's manner of living? Certainly within the laws of mathematics, populations in all species naturally increase over time. But by exempting our species from the natural boundaries and ethical foundations of food cycles, balance, and sustainability, we may well have fostered conditions that promote the current situation of *Homo sapiens* population spinning out of control. Consider the following statistics:

- For the first 200,000 years of existence, *Homo sapiens* population expanded bit by sustainable bit, hovering around 20 to 40 million.

Then the mutiny began.

- By 1600 BCE, there were 100 million *Homo sapiens* on Earth.

- By 200 BCE, 200 million.

- Over the next 1,200 years our population rose to 400 million.

- By 1706 CE (when Benjamin Franklin was born), there were 750 million people on Earth.

- Then, only 200 years later (1900 CE), it had doubled to 1.5 billion.

- By 1960 CE (sixty years later), the year John Kennedy was elected president of the United States, there were 3 billion members of *Homo sapiens* on Planet Earth.

- And now only fifty years later, in the year 2010 CE, Earth's human population has soared to over 6.6 billion women and men, moms and dads, grandmas and grandpas, and boys and girls.

These numbers represent a staggering increase. What does the near future hold? What has this relatively recent population explosion done to the evolving Tree of Life? The future is cause for disquiet. Unless the garden experiences massive premature deaths of 1 billion, 2 billion, or even 3 billion human beings in the next several years, our population will conservatively skyrocket to around 9 to 10 billion in the next four decades, and 14 to 16 billion by the end of this century. Problems of pollution, species extinction, crime, prison overflow, depression, addiction, waste, distrust, government surveillance, "designer" or pre-emptive warfare, water shortage, and soil depletion will increase exponentially.

Can the community of life withstand such an out-of-control expansion of one species? For that matter, can we humans stand that many of our own kind? Probably not. Again, populations often naturally increase over time. However, Cain's disregard for God's ways has helped to bring us to this point of emergency. By exempting ourselves from the principles of food cycles, balance, and sustainability, and by casting to the wind any significant measure of personal or national self-regulation, we have de-evolved into a threatening organism, multiplying without regard and consuming without boundary (which is how some cancerous cells operate).[47]

Members of *Homo sapiens* have gotten away with these esca-lating circumstances for several millennia. However, we can't get away with it much longer. The data is undeniable. What current generations are bequeathing to future generations is not only careless, it is chilling. However, when faced with such information, Cain's self-absorbed thinkers usually say things like this:

- I'll be dead by then, so I'm not going to worry.

- I have money (property, possessions, or military), so this will happen to other people, not me or mine.

- Doesn't my ability to destroy Abel show my superi-ority? If Abel is so great, why is he dead and not me?

- If whales, gorillas, and wetlands are so precious, why are they going extinct and not humans?

- And finally, isn't a spectacular life of glory, however brief, homicidal, or suicidal, better than living as a

---

47. In *The Party's Over*, Richard Heinberg makes a compelling correlation between the recent population explosions of the past 150 years, and the discovery of fossil fuels (coal, oil, natural gas). He argues that these fuels have profoundly affected food production—tractors, fertilizers, herbicides and pesticides, shipping, artificial additives to soils and foods—fueling an artificially high population growth rate from less than 2 billion in 1900 CE to more than 6.6 billion in 2010 CE. Since fossil fuels are nonrenewable, and will become scarcer and eventually run out over the next century, it will be interesting to see how this "bubble" of 4 billion people will be affected.

But food is not the only concern. In effect, fossil fuels have almost single-handedly triggered the Industrial Age. These energy products have enabled the discovery and extrication of countless minerals and biological resources. They are used in heating and cooling systems, modes of transportation (trains, planes, and automobiles), and a myriad of everyday derivative fossil fuel products: computer chips, dishwashing liquids, paint brushes, insecticides, deodorants, tires, linoleum, refrigerator linings, floor wax, glue, roller-skate wheels, trash bags, hand lotion, dyes, soft contact lenses, shampoo, cameras, food preservatives, ink, CDs, ammonia, movie film, rubbing alcohol, fertilizers, credit cards, water pipes, golf balls, guitar strings, antihistamines, nail polish, carpeting, and parachutes, to name only a few.

mere gracious participant and wise steward of God's evolving Tree of Life?

Cain's views are fairly mainstream in Taker cultures, sometimes in behavior, sometimes in rhetoric. Listen to talk radio. Watch most corporate-owned news programs, the Discovery Channel, and even some religious broadcasting. You'll often hear either gleeful championing or helpless resignation regarding the "real world" of Cain's ways. According to sources like these, this just must be the way things are meant to be.

The contrast is clear. While Abel adopts an ethic of regard for the water, soil, and air, as well as respect for God, the whole community of life, and for future generations, Cain's focus is on the self, on immediate opportunities for exploitation, and on an insatiable quest for more and more. While Abel champions energy conservation with a careful eye toward keeping pollution to a minimum for the sake of the whole community of life, including future grandchildren, Cain promotes the continued use of fossil fuels and other resources at whatever rates the market dictates. Cain believes that technology will solve whatever tribulations we leave our grandchildren. Pollution should be considered a problem only if it solely affects our own species—or for some, our own nation—now. And while Abel understands that high-density human population is bad for the carrying capacity of the land, Cain sees population growth as a necessary and desired benefit that keeps the economic engine ever running, and the economy ever increasing.[48]

---

48. Rather than practicing water conservation, some communities are betting on desalination systems to convert seawater to freshwater. This may be wishful thinking. The desalination process burns tremendous amounts of energy. Marine life is threatened by the substantial intake forces. And no one has figured out what to do with the discharge of salty brine (tailings). It is too concentrated and toxic to put back into the ocean. Both piling it and burying it will harm biomass, aquifers, and soil.

The lifestyles of almost everyone have now become so enmeshed in the financial, political, and religious machine that daily grinds out Cain's Taker ways that everyone feels hopelessly trapped in this mire. We need a radical change for the sake of God's Earth. We will address this in part IV.

Chapter 7
All Creation Groans

In the relatively brief moment of time since Cain's rise some 6,000 to 10,000 years ago, and the biblical storytellers' encounter with that rise several thousand years later, a culture of Takerism has now spread far and wide. Beginning in the Fertile Crescent and perhaps several other locales, it has swelled into southern and northern Europe, into Asia and the Oceanic Islands, into the Americas, and recently even back into Africa whence *Homo sapiens* first came. Takerism has become so widespread, so dominant, and so domineering, that it has become accepted wisdom and theology to conclude that the species itself, not just this one out-of-control culture, is fatally flawed. That is, human nature compels Cain to destroy God's garden. Nearly all of humanity is part of a homicidal/ suicidal machine hurling the community of life headlong toward eventual calamity, and it can't seem to stop. Addicted to prosperity, we know not how to self-regulate.

"Addicted to prosperity" is Brian McLaren's phrase. By it he means that "we act as though the resources we consume are infinite, and the wastes we deposit are invisible."[49] Like any addiction, this addiction positions people farther and farther from reality.

Around the world, Cain is entrapped in a global economic system (and totalitarian capitalism is just as destructive as totalitarian socialism) that requires expansion in order to stave off collapse. Growth requires expansion. Expansion requires ever-increasing consumption. Cain's citizens are encouraged to spend and spend, use and use. Cain's businesses and governments feel compelled to produce and produce, pollute and pollute. When there is a financial downturn, or even a global economic meltdown, as occurred in late 2008 and through 2009, the mantra of Cain's leaders is "Dig more, grow more, drill more, manufacture more, ship more, and spend more." Twentieth-century theologian Reinhold Niebuhr (1892–1971) captured the pattern this way: "We have thus far sought to solve all our problems by the expansion of our economy."[50] His cautioning words are just as true today.

With the boundless expansion also comes the frantic struggle to cover up the foul effects of overconsumption. That is, facades must be erected. We must encourage people to focus not only on diversions such as foreign enemies or contaminated imports, but also on entertainment in its various and sundry forms. Such distortions contribute to personal disorders such as addiction, obesity, broken families, abuse, ulcers, hypertension, crime, and depression. They also often produce public disorders such as greenhouse gases, mainstream pornography, the military-industrial complex, corporate crime, the spread of hormone-disrupting chemicals into the water systems, the dumping of garbage into the sea, and an ever-expanding prison industrial

---

49. Brian McLaren, *Everything Must Change*, 130.

50. Reinhold Niebuhr, *The Irony of American History*, 29.

complex.[51] It breeds mistrust. It even generates a favorable incli-
nation toward the design, manufacturing, and deployment of
weapons of mass destruction (WMDs), which are the ultimate
assault against God, against creation, against God's ethical foundation, against the Tree of the Knowledge of Good and Evil, and
against the Tree of Life. Currently, nine nations serve as agents
of Cain in this regard.[52]

---

51. At the end of 2007, one in one hundred U.S. citizens were incarcerated.

52. Five nations currently maintain WMDs aimed at God's community of life.
     They are the following: United States, since 1945 • Russia (successor to the
     Soviet Union), since 1949 • United Kingdom, since 1952 • France, since
     1962 • People's Republic of China, since 1964 • Further, three nations have
     conducted WMD tests: India (1974), Pakistan (1980s), N. Korea (2006). •
     Israel is widely accused of possessing secret WMDs but refuses to confirm
     or deny this accusation to the community of nations. • Iran and Syria have
     been accused of exploring the possibility of developing WMDs. • South
     Africa formerly had WMDs but has since voluntarily disassembled them. •
     By 1996, the WMDs of Belarus, Kazakhstan, and the Ukraine were transferred
     to Russia. • The United States shares WMDs with Belgium, Germany, Italy,
     Netherlands, and Turkey. • Canada ceased sharing WMDs with the United
     States in 1984, and Greece followed suit in 2001.

Chapter 8
Feeding Jabba

Throughout billions of years of the Earth's existence, only one portion of only one species has ignored God's ways so significantly. However, at the start of the twenty-first century CE, Cain now wages warfare not only against God's reign, against the Creator's garden, and against Abel, but also against fellow Taker nations. Takerism has become a bloody competition between nations as new and innovative inducements for consumption and pretexts for war are fashioned, marketed, and defended.

As in sixteenth-century colonialism, Cain today wages war against Abel and fellow Cains for geopolitical advantage, financial market dominance, cheap labor, and access to natural resources, especially those beneath the ground of poorer nations. In the sixteenth century, the offending colonial powers included Holland, Great Britain, Portugal, Spain, and France. Today Cain operates through such entities as Britain, China, United States, India, Russia, Germany, Saudi Arabia, Israel, France, Japan, and

Dubai, among others.

The effects are gargantuan. Each nation operates as "a great mobile tub of muscle and suet," words describing Jabba the Hutt from the George Lucas *Star Wars* films (or Pizza the Hutt from the 1987 Mel Brooks spoof called *Spaceballs*). Obsessed with prosperity and unraveled by inner insecurities, Jabba is ravenous. He can't get enough. His belly cries out for more, even as such gluttony renders the spirit less satisfied and the body politic feeling ever more insecure.

There are many Jabbas. Most Jabbas have been incapable of concealing the ugliness of their overconsumption. Other Jabbas, however, have become more sophisticated. Political spin, plastic surgery, and even health clubs are the modern decoys and diversions that allow for continued concupiscence (gathering all things unto oneself) while still allowing people to maintain nice figures, so to speak. Entertainment especially is huge. Consider the NBA, movies, the music industry, Las Vegas, gossip magazines, computer games, pornography, *American Idol*, state-sponsored lotteries, 200 cable TV channels, the Super Bowl, super star salaries, MySpace, Facebook, "reality" shows, the vacation industry, mindless commercials, and more. A visitor from outer space would surely note the large quantities of time, skill, and money Taker cultures invest in entertaining themselves. Entertainment certainly has a legitimate place in God's garden. It adds enjoyment and recreation to living. But when is it over-the-top? When is it a drug that inspires drowsiness? In a Taker culture, such outlets can easily become a destructive diversion from reality, from truth seeing and truth telling, and from realizing God's intentions for the garden.[53]

---

53. This appears to be the burning concern of the Hebrew prophet Amos. "Woe to those who lie upon beds of ivory, and stretch themselves upon their couches, and eat lambs from the flock, and calves from the midst of the stall (veal); who sing idle songs to the sound of the harp, and like David invent for themselves instruments of music; who drink wine in bowls, and anoint themselves with the finest oils, but are not grieved over the ruin of Joseph" (Amos 6:4–6).

Cain has even discovered ways to ship toxins, out of sight and out of mind, to poorer nations, insuring that *their* soil, air, water, and citizens are spoiled, not Cain's. Takerism knows no boundaries. Takerism knows no shame.

To protect Jabba's interests, Cain countries, like ancient Egypt under Pharaoh (as told in the book of Exodus) and the fourth-century Roman Empire under Constantine (c. 271–337 CE), have learned how to effectively utilize what Daniel Erlander, in *Manna and Mercy,* calls the twin arms of military and priest-hood.[54] These servants of Cain are alive and well today, too.

We can see them at work in our own military system. Military recruits in the United States sincerely believe that their honorable purpose is to help those who can't help themselves. They believe they are being called on to defend the safety and legitimate interests of the United States, to protect fellow soldiers, and to serve humanity. Some even consider their service a calling from God. This is what the recruitment ads imply, and many people serving in the military, especially those serving in the lower ranks, honestly consider this to be the truth. And in fact, such noble causes are at times the mission and effect of the U.S. military system.

However, a larger reality is also at work. The military-industrial complex, Dwight D. Eisenhower's (1890–1969) discerning observation, is also a powerful arm of Cain, of Takerism. Here is an excerpt from President Eisenhower's 1961 Farewell Address:

> We annually spend on military security more than the net income of all United States corporations. This conjunction of an immense military establishment and a large arms industry is new in the American experience. The total influence—economic, political, even spiritual—is felt in every city,

---

54. Daniel Erlander, *Manna and Mercy*, 4, 23, 35.

every statehouse, every office of the federal government. We recognize the imperative need for this development. Yet we must not fail to comprehend its grave implications. Our toil, resources and livelihood are all involved; so is the very structure of our society. In the councils of government we must guard against the acquisition of unwarranted influence, whether sought or unsought, by the military-industrial complex. The potential for the disastrous rise of misplaced power exists and will persist. We must never let the weight of this combination endanger our liberties or democratic processes.[55]

This military-industrial complex is an arm of might that leverages the world's markets, resources, political will, and information (do we really believe "intelligence gathering" is just about terrorists?) in Cain's favor. It is an arm of overt and covert presence, as well as subtle or not-so-subtle coercion, which serves to ensure access to the world's resources and dominance of the world's markets. The military in this sense is a servant of Cain.[56]

It can even be argued that the military-industrial complex itself has become its own beast, a thinking, breathing, feeling and consuming creature that requires warfare in order to feed its appetites and justify its expansion. It's no accident that these industries are located in just about every congressional district in the country, and that their lobbyists in Washington, D.C., are legion and legendary. This makes it nearly impossible to control expansion. In addition, arms dealing into nations around the world is not only a lucrative business for many corporations, creating enticing profits for stockholders, it also has the effect

---

55.   Jerome B. Agel, *We, the People: Great Documents of the American Nation*, 313.

56.   The reach of the U.S. military extends into 132 countries. Would we allow other nations to do the same? Add to this the number of military installations inside Israel, Afghanistan, Iraq, and countries who keep the extent of the U.S. military presence secret. I would argue that such muscle holds sway for the sake of feeding Jabba. "Gunboat diplomacy" is not just a quaint term from the Theodore Roosevelt presidency (1901–1909).

of exacerbating and escalating the level and carnage of local conflicts.

We could benefit from reflecting on the role of logic in warfare, or the lack thereof. When common sense teaches that for every "enemy" killed ten more are created from the "collateral damage" alone, and for every problem solved a thousand more are spawned, how is the mathematical inevitability regarded? Is Cain addicted to chaos? Does Cain need war to feel important? Perhaps Cain is like a child from an alcoholic family system who only feels normal and useful in situations of chaos and crisis, who actually sabotages tranquility. Or maybe the feeling of power itself is addictive.

During the panic of 2002 and 2003, as the Bush-Cheney administration[57] and the news media orchestrated the case for war (now known to be unsubstantiated and based on significant false accusations), and as the deployment of troops and equipment along the Iraqi border became complete, it would have taken a leader of wisdom and courage to resist taking the next step. Weapons makers needed to test their products, soldiers needed to vent vitality, politicians needed to appear patriotic, civilian industries had to sell goods and services, universities had grants to collect, and spy agencies had information to disseminate, much of which turned out to be exaggerated, if not fabricated. With the folly of groupthink firmly in place, Bush-Cheney-Rumsfeld-Powell-Rice easily took the next tragic step

---

57. One of the character traits of Jabba is an affinity for torture, which President George W. Bush and Vice President Richard Cheney apparently authorized during their administration (2001–2009). Since leaving office, Cheney continues to argue that torture works, and that the United States, our allies, and our enemies should use it as needed.

igniting the terrors of warfare upon the people of Iraq.[58]

And the news media had an opportunity begging to be exploited. Never mind that the fear of appearing unpatriotic, or of being accused of not supporting the troops, often caused journalists to regress into a kind of "spokesmodel for governmental spin" role. Tom Fenton of CBS News writes about this in his book *Bad News: The Decline of Reporting, the Business of News, and the Danger to Us All.* Never mind that reporters were strategically em*bed*ded (italics added to emphasize a blurring of professionalism) by the military, often resulting in a skewing of objectivity. And never mind that ratings and profits soared. The news media was excited, its members aroused, and its programming possibilities ignited.

In the frenzied world of twenty-four-hour news shows, the drama of "rockets' red glare" and "bombs bursting in air" is a tantalizing storyline for Cain. It makes for gripping TV. It decides careers. It creates a forum in which to appear patriotic and provides endless fodder for radio and TV talk show hosts. It generates enviable profits. While people who work in the news media are just ordinary Cains, no worse or better than the rest of us, one can understand how the interests of commercialism finds almost irresistible the thrilling preparation, ever-looming possibility, horrific actuality, and unsettling wake of the war-

---

58. Years later, not only have American soldiers and their families suffered because of this choice, but several hundred thousand Iraqi citizens have also lost their lives. Countless others have had their limbs severed, bodies crushed, and minds damaged. Think of the implications for decades. Massive "shock and awe" attacks shattered infrastructure (sewer, water, and electricity), institutions (health care, schools, and museums), the economy, and home life. Two to three million refugees were created. In the aftermath, women and children suffer the most in war zones. Crime, family violence, and rape skyrockets. Emotional and mental traumas scar a generation of children. God's garden is trashed beyond decency. Along with massive unfunded financial outlays, the negative effects of this war will ripple through the lives of individuals and families for decades.

making enterprise. It has become bread and butter.[59]

Through the years the military establishment, with the news media often serving as its unknowing and knowing accomplice, has become ever more effective in leveraging the world in Cain's direction and serving as an unwitting arm of Takerism.

Besides the military enterprise, the other arm of Cain, unfortunately, is religion—or rather, the use of religion. There are many religions in the world, and each contains a spectrum of diverse theologies within it. This is certainly true of Christianity, which ranges from fundamentalism through mainline Protestantism and Catholicism and Eastern Orthodoxy, through the ins and outs of various denominations, nondenominations, sects, offshoots, television and radio franchises, publishing companies, and beyond.

Christianity began as an Abel movement, birthed by the life, teachings, healings, counterculture actions, crucifixion, death, and resurrection of Abel (Jesus) of Nazareth. It took root as a Leaver movement trying to combat Takerism's growing dominance. Just as Jesus in a lifestyle of words and actions proclaimed

---

59. An equally unsettling question must be, Why does the public so willingly consume news media products? Why do we fall for the reporting of war propaganda, of half-truths, and of outright lies?

In another era, the Nazis dominated Germany. Why were they so successful at getting regular people to commit atrocities? How could ordinary citizens have grown so disconnected from the community of life, to say nothing of their humanity? And where did all that evil go after the war? Did it disappear? Go underground? Certainly Hitler was a monster, along with Himmler, Rosenberg, Goebbels, Eichmann, Borman, and others. Certainly the dedicated Nazi leadership was heinous, including the SS, death-camp commanders, propagandists, medical researchers, and bureaucrats. But their effectiveness would have been negligible if ordinary citizens, religious institutions, and the media of that time hadn't swooned over the patriotic rhetoric, spoken respectfully of the inane orders, closed their eyes to reality, and carried out the inexcusable terror. Obeying orders that go against God's ethical foundation is never honorable.

the reign of God for the sake of the whole community of life (as opposed to the reign of Caesar for the sake of Rome primarily, or the reign of *Homo sapiens* for the sake of humans primarily), saying, "Repent, for the reign (kingdom) of God has come near (Matthew 4:17)," so the acknowledgment of this reign was to be central to the saving message of his followers. In Matthew chapter 10, Jesus instructs the movement, "As you go, proclaim the good news, 'The reign (kingdom) of God has come near'" (10:7). And though the way God reigned in Jesus was new, the reign of God itself was not.

But over the past 2,000 years, Cain has become particularly adept at drawing Christianity away from its source, at usurping the movement that Jesus began. Not long after Jesus' death and resurrection, much of the Christian community began to move away from the Abel Jesus and merge into Cain's growing sphere of influence, in effect producing a Cain Jesus. The Roman Emperor Constantine in the fourth century played a pivotal role in this switch in at least three ways. First of all, he militarized Christianity. He transformed the Prince of Peace, who even in his own hour of grave danger forsook killing and force as ways to solve problems, into a champion of conquest. During both Constantine's time and since, crosses have been engraved on military equipment, crusades have been waged, and presidents have received military memos framed with Bible verses.[60]

Secondly, Constantine, whose conversion helped transform the Christian movement from an underground and often illegal sect into a privileged and sometimes coercive religion of the state/culture, was instrumental in facilitating the ordering, compartmentalizing, and, I would argue, domestication of the movement. Referring to the variety of theologies and options in those early years, Barbara Brown Taylor writes:

---

60. It has been reported and confirmed that former Secretary of Defense Donald Rumsfeld used this method when presenting his policies, knowing that Bible verses would help him gain leverage with then President George W. Bush.

For almost three centuries these choices existed in wild disarray. Then the emperor Constantine, in his imperial wisdom, understood that a faith with no center would never anchor his crumbling empire. So he called all the bishops together, fed them lunch, and asked them to say something definitive about the nature of God in Christ. He asked them to sort through the choices and agree on one that the Christian church could go forward with. This required many more lunches and some theological bloodletting as well; but, when the bishops had finished crafting a central confession of Christian faith, those who did not choose this option became known as heretics.[61]

And thirdly, Constantine helped meld the faith of Jesus to Cain's growing assault on God's garden. In his book *The Party's Over*, Richard Heinberg describes the deforestation of Europe.[62] In the fourth century CE, lush forests covered nearly 95 percent of Europe and were integral to daily living. Forests were home to creatures great and small, including humans. Wood from trees provided fuel for heating and cooking, timber for building houses, roofing materials for storage facilities, planks for designing watercraft, and lumber for creating tools like spinning wheels and wine presses. The forest ecosystem was central to the lives of the inhabitants of that region, affecting everything from climate to poetry, from trade to survival.

As one can imagine, sacred stories involving trees and forests had developed in hundreds of Abel cultures over the ages. There were forest legends, often including certain frightening or redemptive mythological forest creatures. There were religious rites involving tree spirits, sacrifices, healings, and prayers. There was mystery, there was danger, and there was spirituality.

---

61. Barbara Brown Taylor, *Leaving Church*, 176.

62. Richard Heinberg, *The Party's Over*, chapter 2.

As a more Cain-like version of Christianity took hold, these indigenous tree-related beliefs and rituals came to be labeled as "pagan." New Cain-like understandings began to paint people who held these beliefs, as well as the forest itself, as under the spell of darkness, enticement, and mystery, tainted by ghosts and demons, and backed by superstitious myths. For many, then, it seemed reasonable to conclude that it was the Christian duty to clear the land, push back the chaos, tame nature, and make space and place for the clear, pure light of Christian civilization to break out. By 1600 CE, Europe had gone from a 95 percent forest covering to 20 percent. Surely Abel cut trees as needed for living. But as Christianity blended with Cain, cutting down trees became a hallowed mission, providing religious underpinnings and sanction for Cain's already significant war against God's garden.

These are some of the ways that the emperor Constantine transformed Christian faith into what I suggest is the "other gospel" that St. Paul warned about so vehemently in Galatians 1:6–8, and that Christian history has deposited at our feet in our time.

Thankfully, there has always been a small but faithful remnant of Abel Christians. In recent years, some Takers are beginning to return to the values, way of living, and mission of Abel of Nazareth. Theologies of creation-care are making a comeback. Earth-stewardship is now given the serious attention it deserves. However, while commendable, one still notices the enduring ideology of human exceptionalism at work. We hear things likes this: while we should care for the community of life out of obedience to God, or for the sake of our children's future, or for commercial, recreational, or even aesthetic reasons, in the end we should not be overly concerned about the garden *per se*. It is just a thing, after all. It is an object, made for us. In fact, to have undo regard for something so material might be leading us down a slippery slope toward idolatry, that is, worshipping the created instead of the Creator. In this sense

Cain's version of Christianity has helped solidify Cain's notion of human exceptionalism.

Cain has also used Christianity's notion of Original Sin to soften our surprise at the accumulating crisis in God's garden. According to Cain's Christianity, humans can't help but destroy. It is predictable; it is inevitable. It's human nature, after all. Because of Original Sin, members of *Homo sapiens* are either congenitally sinful, or at least sin inclined. Or else we are hopelessly tainted by this corrupt and futile world by virtue of being born into it and living in it lo these many years. Either way, efforts to live a *radically*[63] new life of sustainability are considered misguided. Such efforts, while enchanting on an individual level, are ultimately naive, possibly arrogant, and maybe even dangerous if we try to live them communally, nationally, or globally. According to Cain, it's best to let "human nature" take its course.[64]

At their core, the theologies of Cain believe that Takerism represents the fated condition of all of humanity, rather than one aberrant and now dominant culture within humanity. These theologies consider Takerism to be basic to human makeup, and irreversible in this life. Therefore, the Christian religion should *not* be about the business of helping people to live honorably within the community of life. Rather it should be concerned

---

63. Shane Claiborne writes that the word "radical" itself means "root." It's from the Latin word *radix,* which, just like a radish, has to do with getting to the root of things (*The Irresistible Revolution,* 20). Cain is adept at fostering the superficial appearance of things and preserving the prevailing cultural myths, most of which come through the news media venues owned by Cain's companies. Cain fears people getting to the root.

64. Some commercial interests are already gearing up to capitalize on the melting of Earth's ice caps because of global warming. They see it as an opportunity to create new shipping lanes and access new and exotic sea foods and natural resources currently beyond our reach.

with providing passageways of escape from this broken world for individual believers. Such portals of salvation, in the form of spiritual pleasure or miracles in this life, and heavenly paradise after death, enable true believers to be spared from not only the consequences of their own Taker lifestyle, but also that of their neighbor's, their enemy's, and their nation's. This doctrine of sin has become an accomplice to the Taker way of life.

In short, Cain's theology allows Cain to circumvent accountability for the way his Taker lifestyle, personally and nationally, continues to trump and trample God's community of life. He can blame human nature, not human know-how. Adam blames Eve, Eve blames the serpent, and Cain blames human nature. To go against this traditional notion is a scandalous idea for many Christians to consider. It opens the possibility that all of humanity is not by nature sinful. It suggests we are not destined to bring destruction to each other, ourselves, and a significant portion of God's community of life. It suggests that Cain's worldview is actually newfangled in the long, long history of *Homo sapiens*. It suggests that the Creator has been and is fairly pleased with Abel *Homo sapiens*. Admittedly, this concept is very challenging for those trained in Western Christianity, myself included. But I'm getting there.

Further, Cain has also used doctrines of the parousia, or the second coming of Jesus, to teach Taker ways. For Cain, whether the notion of Earth's destruction was intended from the beginning or came after the Fall, this destruction is now central to God's divine plan. God wishes to destroy the world. In fact, we might well pray for the destruction to come sooner rather than later, so that a new heaven and a replacement Earth can arrive. In other words, according to this thinking, to assist in, or at least to not stand in the way of this destruction, may be the faithful thing to do. It's all passing away anyway.

And even among progressive Christians, there is often a presumption that the creation is presently deficient and not whole, and that by God's design it is moving toward a new day of fulfillment. But such eschatological leanings toward a final consummation somewhere off in the future can make one discontented with what has been, and indifferent toward what is. Such a worldview can become just another addiction, this time to the future (or to the novel, or to the something "other"). But really, what is evolutionary advancement or success? Is a horse today more advanced than a horse was 50 million years ago? They are certainly different, but is one better than the other? And are today's humans wiser than our ancestors?

So continuing to eat from (but never digest) God's Tree of the Knowledge of Good and Evil, and armed with the delusory power of military might and the sanctioning clout of domesticated religion, Cain forges on as he wields deadly force over most of creation while lacking the wisdom of God to make his tyranny either beneficial or sustainable.

And the whole of creation, including Abel, groans, as together they pray for the return of God's ways in the garden, that God's will may be done on Earth as it is in heaven (Matthew 6:10).[65]

---

65. I find hope in knowing that Cain's culture has preserved treasures like the Lord's Prayer and the stories of Adam and Eve and Cain and Abel. Despite their continued misconstrual, maybe the fact that they still exist is a hopeful sign that God hasn't given up yet. Grass will always break through cement sidewalks, and stones will shout when tongues are silenced (Luke 19:40).

Chapter 9
Can This Be Fixed?

What is the Creator to do? How can the world be saved?

Over time, God sent many Abels into Cain's culture—prophets, rabbis, sages, martyrs—calling Cain to repentance. The New Testament concept of repentance (μετάνοια in Greek) means to change heart, turn around, and go in a drastically different direction. These Abels called on those who were trying to live apart from God's kingdom to return to the community of life and be healed of their "nature deficit disorder." At times, seeds of response took root and sprouted. Lives were transformed and Cain communities amended. Responsible living showed early signs of returning, causing both the Creator and creation to rejoice.

But Cain's culture was and is tenacious, discovering ever more creative ways to assert the following:

- The Garden is made for humans (some even think the universe is made for humans, to do with it what we desire).

- We must conquer it.[66]

- We must rule it.

- We must use it as we desire and discard the rest as expendable.

- We should not stop our quest to command land, sea, sky, weather, wildlife, bacteria, genes, etc., until this holy mission is fulfilled and creation lies bleeding at our feet— until we have created both God and nature in *our* image.

Remarkably, Cain is so sure of the rightness of his ways that even if they don't work—that is, even if they destroy much of Earth—he feels obliged to persist. It is his story after all, his founding myth and birthright. To relinquish it now would be to dishonor the received heritage. To relinquish it now would be to admit error. In his deepest soul, Cain has moments when he feels his inner sickness and yearns to re-establish connection and affection within the Tree of Life. But then the price is calculated—courage, honesty, relationship with God, and relationship with other creatures. It is deemed far too costly. It involves the confession of sins, which is humbling. It involves accepting forgiveness, which is even more humbling. It involves an amendment of individual, community, and national life. It even involves receiving help from others, including the wider community of life. Such repentance feels entirely too daunting.

Addiction language may be a helpful way of describing Cain's sickness. Addicts are not bad people; they're just addicts.

---

66. When former New Zealand beekeeper Sir Edmund Hillary (1919–2008) died in early 2008, the press described Sherpa guide Tenzing Norgay (1914–1986) and him as the first men to "conquer" Mount Everest. They reached the top in 1953 and came back alive. Having myself trekked in the Annapurna Region of the Himalayas and also summitted six of Colorado's fifty-four "Fourteeners" (those mountain peaks over 14,000 feet), the term "conquer" is quite a stretch. When on such a monstrous glacier, one is a speck. The last thing we've done is conquer. If anything, mountaineers realize how small they are. "Grandiose" is an apt adjective for Cain's delusions. Indeed, the Sherpas in Nepal puzzle over the Western requirement for being at the front of the line, at the head of the pack, on the top of the toppest.

They engage in self-destructive and other-destructive behavior, and can't stop without help. All addictions work similarly. People feel empty. Occasional feelings of emptiness are normal and natural. It's how God made us. It goes with garden living. However, Cain's culture says you shouldn't ever feel empty. If you do, there is something wrong. You need to fix it, you need to take a fix.

For some, the fix is workaholism. For others, it's overeating. For others, it involves alcohol, undereating, shopping, promiscuous sex, mood-altering drugs, computer games, buying what advertisers claim we need, violence, even needing to be around people constantly. Unhealthy fixes take various forms. The common factor is that when you take the fix, it works—for awhile. It brings temporary relief from the emptiness by bringing a high or euphoric sense of well-being. The individual person feels valuable and indestructible.

But because the fix is at root a delusion, and for the purposes of our discussion against the ways of the Creator implanted in God's community of life, this temporary sense of well-being comes with a high price. The next morning brings a hangover—nausea, headaches, credit card bills, imprisonment, or the question, "Who is this person in my bed?" It felt great at the time, but in the morning it feels bad. This triggers even deeper feelings of emptiness and low self-regard, prompting the need for another fix. Too often, addictions develop as a result. The irony is that even though fixes are destroying an addict's life and the lives of those around him, this troubled soul has a hard time imagining any possible replacement for his mood-altering drug of choice.

According to the biblical writers, at one point in the story, the Creator even entered humanity. The Deity emptied itself of status and entered the world's state of affairs as never before. In short, this Abel of Nazareth came to announce the reign of God, as opposed to both the reign of Caesar and the reign of humans. This is a remarkable thing, since the whole community of life, including Abel, had been acknowledging the reign of God for eons and eras. They had to, in order to have kept on evolving. Examples of such thinking are found in the Psalms, including these:

> The high mountains are for the wild goats; the rocks are a refuge for the coneys. You have made the moon to mark the seasons; the sun knows its time for setting. You made darkness, and it is night, when all the animals of the forest come creeping out. The young lions roar for their provisions, seeking their food from God. When the sun rises, they withdraw and lie down in their dens. People go out to their work and to their labor until the evening. O LORD, how manifold are your works. In wisdom you have made them all; the Earth is full of your creatures" (Psalm 104:18–24).

Also:

> Praise the LORD from the Earth, you sea monsters and all deeps, fire and hail, snow and frost, stormy wind fulfilling his command. Mountains and all hills, fruit trees and all cedars. Wild animals and all cattle, creeping things and flying birds. Kings of the Earth and all peoples, princes and all rulers of the Earth. Young men and women alike, old and young together. Let all them praise the name of the LORD" (Psalm 148:7–13).

And also this:

> Let the heavens be glad and let the Earth rejoice; let the sea roar and all that fills it. Let the field exult and everything in it. Then shall all the trees of the forest sing for joy before the Lord; for he is coming, he is coming to judge the Earth" (Psalm 96:11–12).

Earth got it. Abel got it. The Creator certainly did. Cain didn't. So here comes Abel of Nazareth announcing and demonstrating in words and actions the good and true news. To members of a species that had mostly forgotten, he declares as clearly as possible, "The time is fulfilled, the kingdom (reign) of God has come near; repent, and believe in the good news" (Mark 1:15).

In living under the reign of God, this Abel of Nazareth did the following:

- He honored God's ethical design, even to the point of not hoarding his own life.

- He loved God with all his heart, soul, mind, and strength, and his neighbor (the whole community of life, including humans) as much as himself.

- He drew wisdom from the flora of the field, fauna of the forest, fish of the sea, and birds of the air.[67]

- He forsook bloodshed as a wise way to solve problems.

- He taught prayer, truth seeking, truth telling, and the virtue of community.

- He was content with enough.

- He enjoyed the sweetness of living in God's hands.

---

67. Jesus showed a new way of thinking about other creatures and what we can learn from them. I recently discovered the works of Ilan Shamir (www. yourtruenature.com), who produces clothing, books and greeting cards with delightful invitations into the community of life. Here are some samples. I find them obviously playful, quite anthropocentric, but nevertheless, worthy of reflection: • Advice from a lake: Be clear—make positive ripples—look beneath the surface—stay calm. • Advice from a lady bug: Spend time in your garden—be well-rounded—keep family close by. • Advice from a humming bird: Take yourself lightly—keep visits short and sweet—show true colors. • Advice from a deer: Be a good listener—know when to lay low—tread lightly— leap over obstacles. • Advice from a tiger: Be a little wild—keep a watchful eye—have an appetite for life. • Advice from a squirrel: Plan ahead—play in the woods—go out on a limb—stay active.

But Cain was tormented by God's preference for his brother's offerings.[68] He was livid to learn that the Taker way of life he had received from his parents, had invested in, and would one day want to pass on to his children was nothing other than "I-centeredness" (the primal definition of sin). So once again Cain slayed Abel.[69]

When one embraces this "I-centeredness" individually, as a nation, or as a species, the spirit of life soon dries up. Humans become isolated from the community of life, from the Creator, from other humans, and from the self. Cain inhabits a vacuum of disconnection and lack of nourishment, which only leaves him feeling further drained and spiritually empty. Hence, the discontent and unsatisfiable cravings of our age: more food, sex, possessions, and security; more information, prescriptions, technology, and communications devices; more days or months or years added to the end of our lives. More, more, more. It is never enough. Why? Because the empty spirit can only be fed in relationship. And Cain's life has become mostly devoid of relationship.

---

68. "In the course of time Cain brought to the LORD an offering of the fruit of the ground, and Abel for his part brought of the firstlings of his flock, their fat portions. The LORD had regard for Abel and his offering, but for Cain and his offering he had no regard. So Cain was very angry, and his countenance fell" (Genesis 4:3–5).

69. It is illuminating to read the Passion narratives of Jesus in light of what this book is proposing. Especially read Mark 14:1–16:8, or John 18:1–21:25. The powers and principalities of Takerism are doing everything in their power not only to marginalize the reign of God, but also to intimidate those inclined to live according to God's way.

Chapter 10
Cain's Tyranny

Cain's influence as global tyrant is now vast. He has overrun and displaced almost every Abel culture on the six inhabited continents. Until a few hundred years ago, Cain could only see his mastery as righteous and beneficial. Now, as the corrosive wake of his administration compounds, it is evident to everyone with eyes to see and ears to hear that Earth's garden is steadily regressing toward population and pollution impairment.

For generations and generations, members of *Homo sapiens* had followed in the footsteps of their predecessor species and lived adequate lives of accord and sustainability within God's community. On this path they continued evolving. A literal reading of Genesis chapters 1–3 might conclude that humans were created on Friday and by the following Tuesday (or just a few years later), everything went sour. In contrast, the view of this new frame suggests that the Fall, or mutiny, occurred well into human history. It suggests that the mutiny began to occur among a few groups of *Homo sapiens* perhaps some 200,000 years into the *Homo sapiens* story. This is not to say that the Leavers did not at times act in ways that hurt the self and others—with jealousy, killing, lust, and greed. They were not saints or demons. However, because Abel cultures remained deeply interwoven within the community of life, those behaviors were curbed by the laws of nature. Systems of checks and balances were allowed to play themselves out. But once the disconnection of Cain began to take hold, those human behaviors took on a toxicity all their own. The confluence of these behaviors among a few particular strains or cultures of *Homo sapiens*, in a few particular locations of the world, created the perfect storm.[70]

This perfect storm of peril includes totalitarian consumerism, to be sure. Satisfying Jabba's appetites has become mainstream and ubiquitous.

It also includes the persistent insistence that there is only one right way to live, and everyone should live that way. This idea was unheard of before Cain's time, and has put unfathomable stress upon garden life. Think of how many Abel cultures have been destroyed over the centuries in the thoughtless attempt to reeducate them into Cain's culture.[71] God's evolving garden was meant to be creative and diverse. There are thousands of legitimate ways in which to live sustainably and honorably. Both sustainability and honor depend on the complementarity of the needs and requirements of each diverse sector in God's garden. To strive for either hegemony or homogeneity not only destroys culture and inspires inner emptiness, but also de-equips humans who

---

70. Three ingredients—heat, fuel, oxygen—are needed for a forest fire to burn. Take away any one ingredient and the fire goes out immediately. Regarding weather systems, several forces must come together at the same time to produce a catastrophe of such magnitude to be known as "the perfect storm."

71. The independent film written and directed by Georgina Lightning called *Older Than America* (Tribal Alliance Pictures, 2008) portrays one tragic example of Cain's attempt to "reeducate" Abel.

otherwise would naturally know how to live. Abel cultures lose their spirit when they are forced to live Cain's unhealthy way of life.

And the perfect storm of peril includes a near complete ignorance of pre-Cain living. Daniel Quinn calls this the Great Forgetting. (Pages 242 through 257 of *The Story of B* are particularly worth reading, and can be found at www.awok. org/great-forgetting/). In the Great Forgetting, Cain became so disconnected from his "family of origin," that is, the three to four million years of hominid living amongst the wide assortment of creatures in the garden, that he began to think that *life itself* had begun with his own culture's rise.

Ironically, Cain, who was very much a latecomer, has been so effective in disassociating himself from 3.7 billion years of garden living, and so thorough in rinsing away 3 to 4 million years of predecessor species living memory, as well as 200,000 years of *Homo sapiens* Abel wisdom and 70,000 years of modern *Homo sapiens* Abel living, that up until the mid-nineteenth century CE, Cain did not even *know* there was abundant life, including human life, prior to his birth 6,000 to 10,000 years ago. He thought the creation itself began with the arrival of his culture. Conversely, Abel cultures have always intuitively acknowledged Earth's prolonged and wondrous saga, feeling no need to affix dates to those primal and mysterious beginnings. It is sufficient to know that it was a long, long time ago—many moons, many snowfalls, many hunts, and many ancestors back in time.

Only Cain believed that it all began with him. In fact, in 1650 CE, Irish theologian James Ussher (1581–1656), employing a mere literal reading of the Bible, calculated the date 4004 BCE as the moment when the universe began. His computations were accepted in triumph by the religious world and even put into the marginal notes of some editions of the King James Version of the Bible. Some of us smile now, but very little meaningful examination of those figures ensued.

Because much of the past has been lost, making our

knowledge of it scant and our understanding minimal, Cain's culture has tended to consciously and unconsciously reduce or dismiss that history. He imagines life prior to his own culture's rise as shiftless, purposeless, unremarkable, tedious, and dreary. He sees it as mediocre, tortured, not worth mentioning, and brutish. It was unsophisticated, brutal, sadistic, primitive, irrelevant, gloomy, inferior, and filled with superstitions and silly belief systems. At best, Cain surmises that his ancestors were just biding time until they could evolve sufficiently to realize and then lay claim to their intended destiny as rulers and Takers in God's garden.

Of course, some still deny the existence of an evolving Tree of Life, including life prior to Cain. The recently opened $27 million Creation Museum in Petersburg, Kentucky, advocates this young-Earth view, a view shared by the many varieties of religious fundamentalism. This theme park museum, established by the biblical apologist group Answers in Genesis (AiG), insists, along with James Ussher, that God created the universe over a six-day period in or around the year 4004 BCE. They fit Adam and Eve, Cain and Abel, dinosaurs, plate tectonics, diamonds, fossil fuels, Noah's Flood, the Ark, the Ice Ages, the Grand Canyon, and even the light-year vastness of outer space into this 6,000-year time frame.[72]

Much of the fundamentalist brand of Christianity, through radio and TV, homeschooling, tracts and publications, etc., preaches and teaches this scenario. In this view, a literal understanding of the Bible is seen as essential to the integrity of Christian faith. It is fundamental, a non-negotiable. Such an understanding is consistent with their interpretation of what scripture is and what it is not. (See appendix A for a much different understanding of biblical interpretation.)

But there is a greater irony. Though some people continue to doubt the certainty of pre-Cain human existence, even among those who *do* acknowledge it, many continue to

---

72. See "Dinosaurs in the Garden" in *The Christian Century* (February 12, 2008): 22–26.

dismiss it as *pre*history. This is a rather presumptuous term given the short duration of Cain's cultural existence. They deride it overtly or subtly as primitive (and therefore bad). They consider it subhuman (and therefore unsophisticated), unhappy (involving unending toil and hardship), and superstitious (child sacrifices, anyone?). There is the boredom factor (without the Internet, how could they possibly experience learning?). There's hostility, Stone Age drudgery, bloody savagery (maybe even headhunters), or the other extreme, the noble savage. Cain finds it difficult to fathom the possibility that life before his mutiny could have been fine, that people may have been adequately fed, flexible, and expectant. They had families, nuclear and extended. They had shelter, food, and clothing. And of the evidence that has survived, it is clear that they had significant knowledge and useful skills. Ultimately, they must have been sufficiently wise to be able to keep evolving.[73]

But Cain's bias has now so thoroughly infiltrated Cain's world, and is so reinforced through nearly every possible

---

73. The Discovery Channel's *Before We Ruled the Earth: Hunt or be Hunted* (2007) portrays our pre-Cain ancestors as living under the pall of constant terror. They were uncivilized and anxiety-ridden, plagued by illness and immorality. They were the prey of large animals, daily living burdensome and dismal lives of toil and disease. In other words, life was terrible "before we ruled the Earth."

In truth, Leavers no more live on the edge of survival than do rabbits, sparrows, elk, horses, lizards, porpoises, ground hogs, redwoods, or mulberry bushes. Jesus thought the same, saying, Consider the lilies of the field how they grow; they neither toil nor spin; yet I tell you, even Solomon [a Cain if there ever was one, not only with riches and slaves aplenty, but 700 wives and 300 girlfriends too! (1 Kings 11:3)] in all his glory was not arrayed like one of these. But if God so clothes the grass of the field, which today is alive and tomorrow is thrown into the oven, will he not much more clothe you—you of little faith? Therefore do not worry, saying, "What will we eat?" or "What will we drink?" or "What will we wear?" For it is the Gentiles who strive for all these things; and indeed your heavenly Father knows that you need all these things. But strive first for the kingdom [reign] of God and his righteousness, and all these things will be given to you as well (Matthew 6:28–33).

Notice how Cain's version of Christianity will often dismiss this part of Jesus' message as nonsensical.

vehicle, including nursery rhymes; preschool, elementary, and secondary education; homeschooling; the university systems; TV shows and commercials; movies; news reports; religion; the Internet; political discourse; sci-fi and fantasy; and computer games. It is the "air we breathe," to use Daniel Quinn's phrase. Cain's take on Earth's story, humanity's story, and God's story has become all pervasive.

When humans become so cut off from their family of origin (that is, from the evolving Tree of Life), from memory, and from the heritage of the community of life, neurosis ensues. It's visceral; it is systemic. Disconnected from reality and without anchor, humans will dwell in a frightening state of "existential disrepair," suffering from what I identified earlier as a "nature deficit disorder." The twentieth-century Christian theologian Paul Tillich (1886–1965) used the term "dis-ease" to express this state.

The mounting evidence is weighty. How many people from Cain's culture are on antidepressants? How many parents (teachers and researchers, too) note the wild and often daily emotional swings in their youngsters, between over-the-top self-importance (even arrogance) and devas-tatingly low self-regard. People suffer numerous addictions. Families experience child abuse and broken marriages. Phys-ical symptoms include ulcers, heart disease, obesity, cancer, and eating disorders. And while politicians and others want to blame "foreigners" for bringing illegal drugs into Taker cultures, one must ask why Cain's populations are such fertile markets? What void is trying to be countered, what empti-ness filled? Are these and other societal problems just the result of isolated and weak individuals, or are they canaries in the mine shaft, red flags in a way of life gone awry?

At the start of the twenty-first century, garden life is in peril. Its air and soil is sullied, the ozone dangerously depleted, its rivers and oceans fouled. Temperature rise and glacial meltdowns attack sensitive areas of our globe.[74] Over 6.6 billion members of *Homo sapiens* roam the Earth with reasonable (sustainable) and unreasonable (unsustainable) appetites. Underground water tables plummet at disquieting rates. Waste dumps spread wide and high. Industrial poisons seep into the soil as if into a bottomless pit. Irreplaceable resources disappear daily. Whole species become extinct at alarming rates.[75] Takerism, and the ever more intense battle to feed Jabba, has nearly wiped out Abel. Cain now rules the garden. Cain now dominates the air, land, and sea. Cain has fulfilled his passion to rule the Earth.

And the whole of God's creation groans in travail (Romans 8:18–25).[76]

---

74. The exhaust from automobiles, burning forests, energy production, and manufacturing adds ever increasing amounts of carbon dioxide into the air. The oceans are absorbing this CO_2, altering the chemical balance on which much of sea life depends. Specifically, the oceans are becoming more acidic. This especially compromises coral reef and shell structures. At current rates, a catastrophe is forthcoming.

75. The journal of *Science* in October 2008 predicted "of the world's 5,487 mammal species, at least one in four land species and one in three marine species face extinction in the foreseeable future" (reported in *USA Today*, October 7, 2008: 7D).

76. The Abel writers of Genesis knew something was amiss in their Taker neighbors. Though the cumulative effects of Cain's misbehavior took time to become fully manifest, those effects have certainly come to visible fruition in recent centuries. (Actually, it's only been a little over five hundred years since the menace even reached the Americas. See appendix B, *Cain Invades South America, 1532* CE)

    The prophet Hosea echoed this travail during the eighth century BCE: "Hear the word of the LORD, O people of Israel; for the LORD has an indictment against the inhabitants of the land. There is no faithfulness or loyalty, and no knowledge of God in the land. Swearing, lying, and murder, and stealing and adultery break out; bloodshed follows bloodshed. Therefore the land mourns, and all who live in it languish; together with the wild animals and the birds of the air, even the fish of the sea are perishing" (Hosea 4:1–4). Cain would likely interpret this passage to mean that when humans don't treat one another well, the Earth suffers. While that is true enough, Abel might frame the meaning differently. The land, wild animals, birds of the air, and fish of the sea are not just a backdrop for humanity's story, but along with humanity are part of the community of life's story, Earth's story, and God's story.

Finally, from the headwaters of Cain's religious systems and "isms" flows the notion that Earth is not really a proper home for humans. Rather, heaven is our true home and destiny. Earth is just a way station. It is a mere and transitory object, meant to be utilized for as long as necessary and then set aside. It may be an acceptable home for the rest of the community of life, given their inferiority, but not for us. The garden is a thing, a fleeting address, not a habitat for humanity. And when the shadows grow long and the day is finally over, the Earth will pass away anyway as God intended. Then humans will take their rightful place with God in heaven. That is where *we* belong.

Such thinking is common in most branches of the Christian church, and must have emerged early on. But is this really the worldview that Jesus of Nazareth lived? As a Christian, I believe in heaven, but only *after* we have lived a life that blesses life here. If I can't be faithful with God's community of life on Earth, how will I be faithful with God's community of life in heaven?

In Cain's mind, heaven is a place where I can finally "get my way." I will be able to self-indulge in guilt-free I-centered-ness and acquire everything I want. God will reward me with nonstop pleasure and bliss; it will be utopia. But isn't this wrong? If anything, isn't heaven a realm where my individual, national, and species I-centeredness will finally be healed, where I can at long last love and serve others and God? What is more, a follower of Jesus of Nazareth and Jesus the risen Christ is someone who has been set free to dare to live that future life *now*.

Perhaps Cain's ambition is actually to rule heaven also. After all, he felt the need to take over God's job on Earth. Why not heaven as well? Humorously, a scene in the 1989 midlife crisis comedy movie *City Slickers* speaks to this. A leathery, grit-eating, tough-guy cowboy named Curly (played by Jack Palance) dies unexpectedly on a cattle drive. Standing at an impromptu gravesite in the middle of the desert, a ranch hand is asked to say a few words about his ornery boss. As the other cowboys take off their hats and bow their heads in feigned reverence, he offers this prayer, "Lord, we give you Curly. Try not to piss him off." Such is the self-absorbed and contrary mind of Cain.

In part II I've proposed that the biblical Fall itself is historical. The writers of this portion of the book of Genesis wrote the Fall story in puzzled response to the behavior of a neighboring culture(s) that had begun to assert itself over and against other humans, and over and against the community of life. While Adam and Eve are not the first actual humans, their stories represent the arrival of a culture of Takers into their region of the world. In stating that Adam and Eve are not actual people, I realize that I disagree with a literal reading of the words of the apostle Paul. Paul's theological argument comparing and contrasting Adam and Jesus requires that Adam be a real individual. For example, in the book of Romans, Paul states the following:

- Therefore, just as sin came into the world through one man (5:12a).

- For if the many died through the one man's trespass, much more surely have the grace of God and the free gift in the grace of the one man, Jesus Christ, abounded for the many (5:15b–c).

- And the free gift is not like the effect of the one man's sin. For the judgment following one trespass brought condemnation (5:16a–b).

- If because of the one man's trespass, death exercised dominion through that one, much more surely will those who receive the abundance of grace and the free gift of righteousness exercise dominion in life through the one man, Jesus Christ (5:17).

But if, as I am arguing, sin didn't come into humanity and the world through the transgressions of an historical Adam and historical Eve, then what is this story about? When and how did sin appear according to these storytellers? I don't think Christians want to say that "sinful" is the way God created humans. Also, I don't want to say that the notion of "human exceptionalism," which I believe is what the Fall story describes and that has contributed to bringing creation to this current state of disrepair, is natural or inevitable in the evolutionary process. Hence, this new framing. I am attempting to portray a more recent "perfect storm," one that occurred a mere 6,000 to 10,000 years ago, which brought about a new way of thinking. This rebellion began the offshoot path of destruction most humans (but not all) currently pursue. This aberrant way is what the Abel Genesis storytellers in their time and place several thousand years later were describing. Cain thinking had begun to reach them.

The specifics of how it all happened are impossible to ascertain. What is clear is that members of Abel cultures saw themselves as interwoven into the community of life and those of Cain cultures did not. What is clear is the *Homo sapiens* species survived and thrived sustainably for generations and generations and only relatively recently has become a destructive presence that is overrunning the world. And what is clear is that the portion of members of *Homo sapiens* today who for the most part dominate humanity's activity in the world, especially its destructive activity, reflect mostly Cain's Taker values and worldview and very little of Abel's Leaver values and worldview.

And herein lays the indictment. After Cain's very brief rule, equaling approximately 1/400th of the period *Homo sapiens* and our predecessor species have been present on Earth, God's garden has entered a time of peril. Now infecting and representing the vast majority of *Homo sapiens*, Cain's culture is leading humanity, the environment, and the community of life itself to the threshold of calamity. A huge part of the problem is that Cain doesn't see the Fall as a fall at all. Rather, he sees it as liberation. He sees our pre-liberation life of living at the hands of God like all other creatures in God's garden as meaningless, lifeless, stupid, empty, primitive, and subhuman. He embraces his Fall as liberation, as not only a good and necessary differentiation from and rising above all other life forms, but as an advancement forward.[77] Cain agrees with the serpent's enticing prediction that "You will not die. For God knows that when you eat of it your eyes will be opened and you will be as God" (Genesis 3). Cain loves what he sees as emancipation. Cain loves being godlike. Cain presumes that because he eats the fruit he digests it, and therefore is now wise. Cain imagines an ontological status superior to the rest of Earth's inhabitants.[78]

---

77. The laws of sustainability are fundamental to God's garden life. For example, each 100-square-mile plot on Earth can sustain up to a certain number of birds, worms, *Homo sapiens*, pronghorn deer, mice, beetles, etc. If one species takes more than its share, the rough balance becomes contorted and sustainability is compromised. "Stockpiling" is but one human habit that throws off the possibility of sustainability. Cain takes pride in being able to do that and sees it as part of his liberation.

78. Lutheran theologian Dietrich Bonhoeffer (1906–1945), one of the few Christians who actively spoke out against the Nazis in Germany, wrote, "Originally man was made in the image of God, but now his likeness to God is a stolen one. As the image of God, man draws his life entirely from his origin in God, but the man that has become like God has forgotten how he was at his origin and has made himself his own creator and judge." *Ethics*, ed. Eberhard Bethge, 18–19.

Figure 1: "A general timeline highlighting 13.7 billion years."

2,000 years ago	Christianity *begins*
4,000	Judaism
8,000	Cain's culture
11,000	end of most recent ice age
12,000	new forms of agriculture
14,000	Great Lakes formed
15,000	elephants, horses, lions, cheetahs, camels, giant ground sloths becoming extinct in the American West
35,000	Neanderthals die out, only modern *Homo sapiens* left
40,000	evidence of cave paintings, figurines, bone carvings, jewelry, burial of dead
70,000	modern *Homo sapiens*
120,000	Neanderthal *Homo sapiens*
200,000	*Homo sapiens*
780,000	*Homo erectus* migration out of Africa
800,000	fire use among predecessor hominid species
1,900,000	bison in North America
2,100,000	predecessor hominid species use tools to hunt, prepare food, construct shelter
2,500,000	23 successive cycles of ice ages begin, making lakes and rivers
4,000,000	predecessor hominid species (*Australopithecus, Homo habilis, Homo erectus*)
5,500,000	carving of Grand Canyon begins
6,000,000	Mediterranean Sea is dried up salt basin generating Sahara Desert
20,000,000	primates
35,000,000	felines
50,000,000	some land mammals become aquatic (whales, dolphins, manatees)
65,000,000	mammal surge after dinosaur extinction
125,000,000	marsupials (kangaroos and koalas)
140,000,000	plants bearing fruit
195,000,000	mammals
200,000,000	super-continent Pangaea beginning to break up
295,000,000	reptiles (including dinosaurs)
320,000,000	insects first take flight
395,000,000	sea life moves onto land
425,000,000	trilobites, brachiopods, cephalopods, reef systems
543,000,000	Cambrian explosion: burst of life diversity
660,000,000	multiple-cell life (perhaps as early as 1.2 billion years ago)
1,300,000,000	cells develop reproduction
1,750,000,000	single-cell life (eukaryotes, cells with nuclei)
2,300,000,000	oxygen increase from algae
2,700,000,000	photosynthesis
3,700,000,000	single-cell life (prokaryotes, cells without nuclei)
4,600,000,000	Planet Earth
13,700,000,000	our universe

Part Three

Objections: An Intermission

If you've read to this point, you likely have questions and objections. I confess to numerous gaps yet to be addressed in this reconsideration, though less I believe than in the more common renderings of Earth's story, humanity's story, and God's story.

The following are questions and objections that I have come across in discussions with others. Before tackling the urgent and central question of part IV—Is there hope?—I will address these briefly. Certainly these and other objections are honest and will require substantial further exploration. But here is a top-ten list:

Question #1: Does this reconsideration advocate a return to the Stone Age—with no cars, no TVs, no computers, no airplanes, and no mass production of food?

Response: No. The planet could not endure 6.6 billion hunter gatherer *Homo sapiens*. Also, there is much that is good about modern life. The key objectionable word here is "totalitarian," as in totalitarian consumerism, totalitarian socialism, totalitarian capitalism, totalitarian pollution, and totalitarian agriculture. There ought to be a way for humans to partake of what is truly necessary and good without behaving in a manner that destroys the Tree of Life. Perhaps it is just this simple: take what is needed and leave the rest. "Sustainability" is the operative principle.

Of course in Cain's worldview, concepts like "necessary and good" and "leave the rest" are absurd. Who decides what is needed? Who determines what is good? Sustainable for just our species, or for all? And if I leave the rest for another day, won't someone else just take it? These concepts are difficult for Cain to grasp. He sees them as an ominous threat to his economic progress, if not his personal freedom. For Cain, freedom means that the world belongs to him and he should be free to hunt or fish without limit, cut down trees at will, and graze, mine, burn, and kill without concern.

But for Abel, the concept is not that complicated. It's common sense. It is wisdom borne in a cherished relationship with the community of life and with the Creator.

Question #2: How involved is God in the evolving Tree of Life?

Response: This is a question for Cain's framing, too. God's involvement is certainly transcribed into the laws of garden living, as I have argued. Further, I believe God is immanent and in a covenantal relationship with all creatures, including humans, as the writer of the following passage seems to imply:

> God said to Noah and to his sons with him, "As for me, I am establishing my covenant with you and your descendants after you, and with every living creature that is with you, the birds, the domestic animals, and every animal of the Earth with you" (Genesis 9:9–11).

But beyond that, does God intervene? Does the Creator ever suspend the natural and ethical processes of the evolving Tree of Life for a small or large miracle? And into which realities might God intervene?[79]

My own leanings have room for a positive response to this question when intervention is deemed necessary by the Creator for the good of the whole. However, I don't know how to defend this. It is solely a statement of faith.[80] God is internally related to everything, subject to subject, perhaps like lovers influencing one another. I don't mean we are puppets or robots. But there is

---

79. The British mathematician and natural philosopher Isaac Newton (1642–1727) described one form of reality, namely, the visible physical universe. With atoms as the basic building block, this visible reality behaves in machinelike fashion, within a measure of predictability. Drop a rock, it falls to the ground. Push a ball, it moves until countered by gravity.

    But then a new science discovered an additional reality. This smaller than an atom (subatomic) reality is the unseen, though mathematically inferred, world of quantum physics. It is made up of quarks, baryons, leptons, bosons, gluons, fields, and ever smaller particles. Even though it is the reality out of which Newton's world of everyday experience is constructed, this fitful and unseen substrate operates according to laws wildly at odds with Newton's reality. See Barbara Brown Taylor's *The Luminous Web*, especially pp. 47–75, for a fairly clear illumination, from a theologian, no less! One particularly fascinating discovery in the quantum world has to do with light. Is it a particle or a wave? Well, it appears to be both. This phenomenon is not necessarily illogical, but it is certainly curious if not mysterious.

    And, if this isn't confusing enough, Christians and others also speak of a spiritual reality. Again, in what manner and into what realm does God intervene?

80. This raises other serious questions, namely, Why doesn't God intervene whenever there is a severe situation? What kind of God would not fix dire circumstances of suffering if such a thing were possible? Again, I don't know.

too much going on in the visible, quantum, and spiritual worlds for me to believe in pure "free will" either. There is something in between, just "will" perhaps. William Paul Young in his novel *The Shack*, addresses this complexity well:

> "Your family genetic heritage, your specific DNA, your metabolic uniqueness, the quantum stuff that is going on at a subatomic level. . . . Or the intrusion of your soul's sickness that inhibits and binds you, or the social influences around you, or the habits that have created synaptic bonds and pathways in your brain. And then there's advertising, propaganda, and paradigms. Inside that confluence of multifaceted inhibitors," she sighed, "what is freedom really?" (*The Shack*, 95).

Question #3: You always portray Cain pejoratively. This worldview can't be all bad.

Response: The problem is that even when Cain's way of life produces benefits for some humans in the form of extended life spans, opportunities for learning, inventions that raise the standard of living, etc., it is not sustainable for the planet. In fact, even the American dream is a death sentence for the planet if more than the current 5 percent of the world's population tries to live it.[81]

One could even argue that members of the Mafia are in some ways good people. Mafia members take care of family and community and even donate to good causes. They do acts of charity. They show love and concern. But the hard reality is this: Cain is a murderer. He is at war with God, with creation, with Abel, and with other Cains. This habit of warfare is integral to Cain's self-

---

81. The United States represents 5 percent of the world's human population. However, it is responsible for 40 percent of the world's consumption, pollution, and species extinctions. For one nation to take so much more than their fair share is obviously ethically problematic for Christians and others who are searching to be faithful to God.

understanding and worldview, and it is bringing ruin to God's community.

Along with this, we might ask: Why has Cain been so successful in affecting so many? Why couldn't thousands of Abel cultures withstand Cain's onslaught? Imagine for a moment eight people living in the same house. Of the eight, one person carries an assault rifle. This person has low self-regard, and even lower regard for others. He has been known to have a temper, to be violent, and has demonstrated that he has no qualms about using his weapon to get his way. Surely, his willingness to be ruthless will affect the whole community. (See appendix B for a stark example of how much harm even a small number of Cain's agents can inflict.) It is difficult to withstand someone who will go to any lengths to get their way, without resorting to becoming Cain-like, too. Cain may think such success demonstrates his superiority (that is, that might makes right), when in fact, it shows his regressed state before the Creator.

Question #4: What about medical science? Terrible diseases and conditions are being cured every decade. Lives are saved. Must we give this up?

Response: No. Much of this is beneficial and sustainable. However, I wonder if there is also such a thing as *totalitarian* medicine? I wonder about the portion of the cures we discover and the treatments and surgeries we apply that are for diseases that are caused by our Taker lifestyles—diseases like hypertension, heart attacks, ulcers, cancer, asthma, acid reflux, stroke, diabetes, etc.—the so-called modern or Western diseases? For example, salt, fat, and sugar have been scarce commodities throughout most of *Homo sapiens* history. Salt was sequestered underground unless mined (except for those who lived near the sea). Fat rarely existed in lean, healthy wild animals. Sugar was only available in isolated locales. Initially, when these three commodities were first introduced, their high prices restricted their use to the wealthy. However in recent decades they have become inexpensive and readily obtainable. In fact, in our time these relatively unhealthy additives saturate almost every processed food humans eat. They are added effusively in high dosages for taste, for mouthfeel (fat molecules give certain "comfort" textures to foods), and as preservatives. We might ask, To what detriment?

Also, there is an ethical question of cost and priorities. Globally, the rich are extending the life of the rich at an enormous cost. It is not unusual for a single person to spend hundreds of thousands of dollars for their Taker-caused ailments. Is this just? And when does extending the life of the wealthy drain resources from the quality of life for others? What does justice and integrity mean in this context?

Further, pharmaceutical's metabolites, some of which are still biologically active and therefore dangerous, are being introduced as waste contaminants into our water supplies along with the already problematic agricultural and industrial pollutants. This is currently affecting flora and fauna, including humans, and undermining whole ecosystems.

Question #5: What about noble and good people in Cain's culture, those who live Christ's Abel way?

Response: A remnant exists, praise God. God finds ways to infiltrate. There are people like Mahatma Gandhi (1869–1948), Mother Theresa of Calcutta (1910–1997), Martin Luther King Jr. (1929–1968), Dorothy Day (1897–1980), Dom Helder Camara (1909–1999), Desmond Tutu (b. 1931), and numerous ordinary neighbors and strangers who live what would be considered normal and courageous human lives from God's perspective. There are also the Cains, including Cain Christians, who have decided to leave their Taker worldview and live the Abel way. These are the small but significant remnant of the faithful. The world needs them as role models.

But the problem is this: too many of us believe it's possible to be both Cain and Abel simultaneously or intermittently, to serve both God and mammon.[82] In browsing through a copy of *O, the Oprah Magazine* (April 2008), I was struck by the juxtaposition of articles about living "green" next to countless ads and articles promoting excessiveness. One conspicuous example came from *O*'s creative director, Adam Glassman, who on page 112 "tells you what your best friends won't." To someone who was trying to hide her large tummy (from overeating, perhaps?), he advises the purchase of a Tory Burch "well-proportioned tunic with elongating vertical embellishments" for $450, or a Dana Buchman "softly belted scoopneck top" for $275, because "the long tie draws the eye down and away from the midsection." Why not just eat healthier and exercise more, we might ask?

Question #6: Why shouldn't we think of Leaver cultures as primitive and inferior?

Response: Their way of life was sustainable for the planet. Ours is not. They were stewards of the evolving Tree of Life. We are bringing it to ruin. Which culture is more advanced?

To be clear, Abel is not a saint. But neither is he any more harmful than the elephant of Kenya, the cactus wren of the Sonoran Desert, the coati mundi from Costa Rica's rainforest, or the Alaskan brown bear. He has a legitimate purpose within the community of life, just like the Rocky Mountain marmot, the coyotes on the Great Plains, or the pinyon pine and juniper trees in

---

82. Jesus said, "No one can serve two masters; for either he will hate the one and love the other, or be devoted to the one and despise the other. You cannot serve God and wealth," (Matthew 6:24).

the lower elevations, ponderosa pine in the transition zones, and spruce, fir, quaking aspens, and bristlecone trees mantling the higher mountain heights. Abel living doesn't produce sainthood. But it does produce ordinary human beings living in a sustainable and complementary relationship with God's community of life.[83]

The reality is that so much of the record has been lost, including our corporate memory. Writing systems weren't even invented until only a few thousand years ago. Therefore, very little is known about 99.5 percent of human history. Ironically, this 99.5 percent is referred to as *pre*history, and the one half of one percent as history.[84]

Question #7: If Cain even slows or halts the current rates of economic production, consumption, and pollution, won't the global economy collapse?

Response: This is everyone's fear. But think of the incredible amount of time, money, education, and energy currently invested in the direction Cain is taking us. What if those investments were redirected? What if they were rein-

---

83. Daniel Quinn suggests that the Taker world lives inside a prison. Inside a prison there are rich and poor, powerful and weak. The rich in prison can get anything they want. A Donald Trump calls the shots inside prison, and can get anything he wants. Except he doesn't have the key to get out. Some prisoners try to redistribute the power and wealth in prison. Others find so much security and status in prison that they choose to stay. Some Leavers choose imprisonment over extermination on the outside. A well-run prison has a prison industry to keep inmates busy, so they won't get bored or see the futility of their lives. They have entertainment. Consumerism is the entertainment that is the prison industry for Cain. So the real question is, How can Cain and Abel join hands to get out of prison?

84. In the same way that life probably existed millions of years prior to leaving fossilized evidence, since its physiology didn't contain materials that could fossilize (except for certain biomarkers or chemical fossils), so most of the history of *Homo sapiens* has not survived in the historical record. Abel employed mostly perishable and biodegradable items for daily living—wood, bone, antlers, shells, ivory, hide, plant fiber, seeds, nuts, grasses, and plant and animal oils and fats—usually leaving little or no trace. Yet, it would be a mistake to discount their sojourn as nonexistent or insignificant.

vested in the direction of wisdom? Not as charity. Not as an afterthought. Not even as some pet project. But as the central engine of our national interest. What if this is what students learned in business school?[85] What if, after the global economic meltdown of 2008 and 2009, we try to build a sustainable economy instead of rushing to rebuild what we had before? Think of what we could achieve if leadership in government and industry focused on that goal. It may not be such a radical and ridiculous notion after all.

Question #8: What is wrong with polluting first and then figuring out a way to clean it up afterward?

Response: That kind of approach also creates jobs, doesn't it? So what is so terribly wrong with creating businesses that dirty the soil, air, and water, and then creating businesses that clean it up?

The 1987 parody movie *Dragnet* stars Tom Hanks and Dan Aykroyd as detectives. The villain, played by Christopher Plummer, is discovered near the end of the movie to be both running a business that produces vice *and* leading a crusade that fights it. Wouldn't this be a similar thing? Certainly it is better not to cause the harm in the first place.

---

85. When a company develops a line of fair-trade products (coffee, for example) it is very commendable. However we must also ask at some point why the company continues to produce nonfair-trade products. Similarly, if a company develops a way to produce products that are efficient, nonpolluting, sustainable for the planet, and wholesome for the common good, why would that same company also continue to produce products that are inefficient, polluting, unsustainable for the planet, and unwholesome for the common good? Perhaps companies are seeing "green" as one market among many. What if that changed? What if we expected more from our leaders? Cain would argue that it's just human nature to be greedy and destructive. Again I would argue, while greed is one of the options available even to Abel, the wholesale worldview of Takerism is a recent anomaly and not basic to our human nature.

In Abel's world, the worldview and behaviors of an entrepreneur or corporation would coincide with significant ethical principles and would ask questions such as the following: (1) Are we producing goods and services that are wholesome? (2) Do we treat our workers fairly? (3) Is there a modest profit, and do we use it to benefit both our families and the wider community of life? (4) Do we keep the air, soil, and waters clean?[86] Such questions are red flags to Cain. They seem idyllic, subversive, even foolish. But they make perfect sense to God, the community of life, and Abel.

Really, the problem isn't necessarily the quality or quantity of Cain's offering. It's how he got it. Cain's way of earning and spending produces far more damage and destruction than his acts of charity can ever hope to counter. A more generous Cain is not the goal. Charity can never catch up. The goal is for Cain to rejoin the community of life through work, home, and play, and to live sustainably at the outset. Prevention is a whole lot better than treatment.

Question #9: Don't you romanticize Abel living? Surely members of *Homo sapiens* prior to 6,000 to 10,000 years ago were violent too. Along with activities such as hunting, farming, raising children, finding spouses, getting colds, moving to a new location, thinking about life's purpose, and dying, some also fought over territory, hoarded, overfarmed tracts of land, overfished waters, even possibly brought to extinction animals like the saber-toothed tiger, mammoth, and mastodon. Other

---

86. In early 2008, reports circulated about a "great garbage patch," or "trash vortex," in the northern Pacific Ocean. Essentially, it's "a floating expanse of waste and debris" brought together by ocean currents and covering an area the size of the continental United States. This vast spread of "plastic soup" is comprised of tons and tons of flotsam. One-fifth of the junk is thrown off of ships and oil platforms. The rest comes from industrial and household waste on land.

than degree, what really is the difference between the cultures of Cain and the cultures of Abel?

Response: The difference is actually quite vast. The following are several examples:

- Abel sheep and goat herders, for example, certainly found wolves maddening. When their villages or flocks were targeted by a wolf to be its meal for the day, they naturally fought back and tried to track and kill that wolf. However, it would be unthinkable for Abel to intentionally go on a decades-long hunt with the ultimate goal of exterminating the entire species. There was a kinship with wolves, and a respect for them, which can be observed in the stories and artwork of antiquity and the present day.

- Many native cultures in North America depended on the buffalo for their livelihood. This large, shaggy-maned, hoofed mammal numbered an estimated 75 million at one time, with herds stretching from present day Canada to Texas, Utah to Ohio. An entire way of life for native families revolved around this mammal. Timothy Egan writes:

  > Bison gave them just about everything they needed: clothes, shelter, tools, and of course a protein source that could be dried, smoked, and stewed. Some tepees required twenty bison skins, stretched and stitched together, and weighed 250 pounds, which was light enough to be portable. The animal stomachs were dried and used as food containers or water holders. Even the tendons were put to good use, as bowstrings.[87]

  So in order to feed their families and build their communities, native peoples had been hunting the buffalo animal for generations upon generations. One

---

87. Timothy Egan, *The Worst Hard Time*, 16.

hunting strategy even involved enticing part of a herd to plunge off a cliff to their deaths, which sometimes resulted in more buffalo being killed than could be processed. Hence, some waste. Also, because buffalo herds could be dangerous, village planners needed to be smart in choosing sites to avoid an unfortunate encounter with a large herd.

However, it would have been unthinkable for Abel to try to lay waste an entire species. It would have been unimaginable to slaughter herd after herd for sport, for the railroads, or as a weapon of warfare in an equally unthinkable endeavor of exterminating one's tribal neighbors. Such conduct would be incomprehensible to Abel, and could only stem from a puzzling disconnect from the community of life. One can only imagine the bewilderment among native families as they witnessed the flagrant waste and perverse insolence of Cain's killing fields.

- Abel raised chickens, turkeys, cattle, and pigs. They were slaughtered as needed for food and clothing. However, it would be unthinkable to remove the animals from their natural environment and imprison them in crammed cement cells, to be fed with chemicals and processed food injections. Abel would not behave toward a fellow citizen in this manner.

- Finally, in Cain's mind, every square foot of this planet (and for some, of the universe) was made for humans and belongs to humans. The truth of this manifesto has not been doubted by any variation of Cain since the beginning of his culture. As Daniel Quinn points out:

> It wasn't doubted by the builders of the ziggurats of Ur or the pyramids of Egypt. It wasn't doubted by the hundreds of thousands who labored to wall off China from the rest of the world . . . the traders who carried

gold and glass and ivory from Thebes to Nippur and Larsa . . . the scribes of the Hittites and the Elamites and the Mitanni who first pressed the record of imperial conquest into clay tablets. It wasn't doubted by the iron-workers who carried their potent secrets from Babylon to Nineveh and Damascus. It wasn't doubted by Darius of Persia or Philip of Macedon or Alexander the Great. . . . It wasn't doubted by Hannibal or Julius Caesar or Constantine . . . the marauders who scavenged the bones of the Roman Empire—the Huns, the Vikings, the Arabs, the Avars, and others. It wasn't doubted by Charlemagne or Genghis Khan . . . the Crusaders or by the Shiite Assassins . . . the merchants of the Hanseatic League. It wasn't doubted by Pope Alexander VI, who in 1494 decided how the entire world should be divided among the colonizing powers of Europe . . . by the pioneers of the scientific revolution—Copernicus and Kepler and Galileo . . . by the great explorers of the sixteenth and seventeenth centuries—and it certainly wasn't doubted by the conquerors and settlers of the New World. It wasn't doubted by the intellectual founders of the modern age, thinkers like Descartes, Adam Smith, David Hume, and Jeremy Bentham . . . the pathfinders of the democratic revolution, political theorists like John Locke and Jean-Jacques Rousseau . . . the countless inventors, tinkers, dabblers, investors, and visionaries of the Industrial Revolution . . . the industrial giants who built the railroads and armed the armies and rolled out the steel—the Du Ponts, the Vanderbilts, the Krupps, the Morgans, the Carnegies. It wasn't doubted by the authors of the Communist Manifesto, by the organizers of the labor movement, or by the architects of the Russian Revolution . . . the rulers who plunged Europe into the maelstrom of World War I . . . the authors of the Treaty of Versailles or by the architects of the League of Nations . . . the scores of millions who were jobless during the Great Depression . . . those who struggled to establish parliamentary democracy in Germany or by those who ultimately defeated them . . . the hundreds of thousands who labored in an industry of death created to rid humanity of "mongrel races." It wasn't doubted by the millions who fought World War II or by the leaders who sent them to fight. It wasn't doubted by the hardworking scientists and engineers who exerted their best skills to rain down terror on the cities of England and Germany.

The world was made for Man, and Man was made to conquer and rule it.

This manifesto certainly wasn't doubted by the rival teams that raced to split the atom and build a weapon capable of destroying our entire species. It wasn't doubted by the architects of the United Nations. It wasn't doubted by the hundreds of millions who in the postwar years dreamed of a coming utopia where people would rest and all labor would be performed by robots, where atomic power would be limitless and free, where poverty, hunger, and crime would be obsolete.[88]

I would add that it has rarely been doubted by any anthropologist, physician, industrial agriculturalist, historian, inventor, pharmacologist, elementary school teacher, preacher, aerospace engineer, general, or anyone who consciously or unconsciously has become part of Cain's now dominant culture. However, and this is the point of Daniel Quinn's works and my exposition and enlargement of his insights, such an understanding doesn't represent humanity *per se*, but only one significant, large, and dominant cultural grouping within humanity.

---

88. Daniel Quinn, *The Story of B: An Adventure of the Mind and Spirit*, 279–281.

The above examples are not meant to say that Abel was or is perfect, or to say that God isn't concerned with healing and saving the lives of both Abel and Cain. This will be further discussed in part V—Reframing the Christian Story. These examples, rather, are meant to counter the claims of Cain such as the following:

- Humanity has always been Cain-like.

- Cain's culture is simply the next logical step meant to supersede Abel's culture.

- Cain is a more advanced form of humanity.

- It is inevitable that humans will all evolve (or devolve) into Cain.

- It is natural that members of *Homo sapiens* destroy God's world.

In truth, Abel still lives. Cain is a break-off stream flowing parallel to Abel, at odds with both Abel and the greater stream of life. The creation, the Creator, Abel, and even Cain all ache because of the story/narrative that Cain, including Cain Christianity, is enacting.

Question #10: What again is the core meaning of the two trees in the garden?

Response: Humans can only find the Tree of Life and not be the end of creation if they stay in the garden, that is, live under the reign of God among the community of life. And we can only stay in the garden if we keep our hands off of God's domain and rule, represented by the Tree of the Knowledge of Good and Evil. God is not cruel. God is not even trying to deny pleasure in banning access to this tree. It's just that this fruit is poison in human mouths. Its knowledge is too powerful for any creature or species to handle. It is toxic. It is dynamite. Why? Because the knowledge of the Tree is all about life and death—who shall live and who shall die—whether it be the lion or the rabbit, the sea bass or the whale or the parasite, the termite or the tree or the decomposed remains producing coal over millions of years, the flu virus or the cab driver, the hurricane or the fisherman. The playing out of life on millions of levels is under the influence of a competence greater than that of any creature or species. Theologian Reinhold Niebuhr (1892–1971) wrote something similar in 1952 when he said, "Modern man lacks the humility to accept the fact that the whole drama of history is enacted in a frame of meaning too large for human comprehension or management."[89] I can't help but think of a know-it-all thirteen-year-old who is full of himself, equipped with an endless capacity for doing damage, but possessing very little wisdom.

The real danger is not that Adam and Eve actually gain knowledge by eating of the Tree. That's impossible. It's that they imagine they do. By their declaration of independence from God, often under the guise of religion, they imagine they know how to rule the Earth. Cain is deadly because he *presumes* to know what God knows. Being full of what he thinks is godly knowledge, he proceeds to relegate Abel and the wider community of life to the status of the lesser. Cain's cultures are so convinced that this is the truth, that they will commit various forms of genocide toward the wider community of life, including other humans, to prove their

---

89. Reinhold Niebuhr, *The Irony of American History*, 88.

point. Adam and Eve are still chewing on the fruit of the forbidden Tree, and Cain is still hunting down Abel and creation for the kill.[90]

These questions and responses have begun to scratch the surface. Obviously, there is much more to consider. Having presented the first half of this reconsidered narrative, and responded to several of the substantial questions during this brief intermission, we will now explore the question of hope. This is the most important question on the table.

---

90. Perhaps another way to get at Cain's thinking is to listen in on a conversation between two Cains. It might go something like this. "We know humans shouldn't have eaten from the tree. Big mistake. Our bad. Forgive us, Lord. But now that we have eaten, and apparently have replaced our innocence with new knowledge, and of course can never go back, and so are now living in the 'real world' east of Eden"—Cain mistakenly thinks that life before his disobedience was one of innocence, which I'm saying couldn't be farther from the truth— "how are we going to use our new godlike wisdom? We weren't supposed to have it, but now we do. We are godlike creatures whether we like it or not, and therefore are wiser than any other creature, including our unfortunate brother Abel. The question is, How are we going to handle our new responsibility of being rulers of this world? If we don't step up, there will be chaos. We can't let that happen. We must do as much good as we can, and not any more evil than we have to. Perhaps we can even develop various religions that will enable us to ask God to work with us in our new role as rulers."

Again, my point is this: even though Adam and Eve and Cain eat God's forbidden fruit, they don't digest it. They can't, because they are not God. Therefore, they never, ever receive the tree's wisdom. Cain is so dangerous precisely because he imagines he possesses such wisdom. He's like a guy who bought a medical degree online for $25 and began practicing brain surgery. Look out world!

Part Four
Is There Hope?

Chapter 11
Is There Hope?

Daniel Quinn believes that children born 100 years from now are in for exciting lives. Why? Because life as we know it will be over. Either Cain will have largely committed suicide and will be living a shadowed existence in a world choked by the ravages of his own making, or Cain will have so dramatically changed the way he functions that life will now have a future. Either way, Cain's Taker lifestyle will not endure.

If the Cain cancer eludes God's healing and thereby effects extinction upon humanity and other species, life itself will not be totally destroyed of course. Some species will survive Cain's holocaust.[91] And with *Homo sapiens* out of the way, the Creator will perhaps allow another pioneering and trailblazing species to emerge, one that might do a better job.

In the face of this possibility, is there hope?

God put two trees in the garden, one for God and one for all other creatures. For 200,000 years, members of *Homo sapiens* kept their hands off God's tree and partook of the Tree of Life. That is a pretty good track record. Cain's worldview and behavior is a recent abnormality. Thus, thankfully, it does not represent the vast majority of human history. So while the potential for Cain's worldview and behavior is found in human nature, the inevitability of its expression is not. In fact, Cain is such a bizarre anomaly, and so far out of the stream of life, that he can almost be considered an accident.

Is there hope?

Shane Claiborne, in *The Irresistible Revolution: Living as an Ordinary Radical,* sheds light on a passage in Matthew 16:18. Jesus of Nazareth is responding to Peter's confession of faith, saying, "I tell you, you are Peter, and on this rock I will build my church, and the gates of hell shall *not prevail against it"* (emphasis added). In a footnote Claiborne writes:

> Gates were built in the walls around cities to fortify them from outsiders. They were for defensive, not offensive, purposes, so many theologians suggest that when Jesus says the gates of hell shall not prevail against it, he is pointing to the fact that he and the church will storm the gates of hell to rescue those inside."[92]

---

91. I use the word "holocaust" reluctantly. I don't want to detract from the magnitude of the horrific Nazi assault upon Jews, gay and lesbian couples and individuals, handicapped persons, Gypsies, and the millions of people who died trying to fight for and against them. Hitler and the people who carried out these annihilations were an acute and visible version of Cain's madness. However, the word "holocaust" is the only word I can think of that has the weight and perversity to capture the global nature of Cain's historic and current destruction.

92. Shane Claiborne, *The Irresistible Revolution: Living as an Ordinary Radical,* 229.

In other words, Jesus promises that God will use the faithful Abel remnants of the church and world to seep through the protective armor of Cain's defended hell to rescue Cain inside. God will unlock the prison doors and set Cain free. Perhaps it's like blades of grass eventually breaking through the cement sidewalk. The Creator is on the side of life.

Is there hope?

Barbara Rossing, in *The Rapture Exposed: The Message of Hope in the Book of Revelation,* reminds us that God loves *this* world. In contrast, writers Tim LaHaye and Jerry Jenkins portray in the popular *Left Behind* book series the view that the destruction of Earth is something not only to be anticipated, but also desired. While unbelievers will perish, the storyline goes, believers will escape the consequences of their poor stewardship. They will not perish. They will be taken some-place else. They will get a new Earth somewhere—perhaps on another planet, in another dimension, or on a magically restored Earth here.[93]

In contrast, God's story says something quite different. "The Earth is the LORD's and the fullness thereof," proclaims the psalmist (Psalm 24:1). And again, "The LORD reigns; let the Earth rejoice" (Psalm 97:1). God is all about the sustenance of the community of life. Humans are called, invited, commanded to participate in that sustenance. Referring to *The Chronicles of Narnia* by C. S. Lewis, Rossing notes that the world we are

---

93. The "Left Behind" views of Tim LaHaye and Jerry B. Jenkins are a recent invention. Actually this theology was constructed in mid-nineteenth century England by John Nelson Darby, a disaffected Anglican priest. These views were promoted in the Scofield translation of the Bible and became the basis of Hal Lindsey's 1970s rapture fantasy book entitled *The Late Great Planet Earth.* Theologically and biblically, Lindsey's views, and current manifestations of it in people like Texas fundamentalist John Hagee, as well as LaHaye and Jenkins, are thin soup in my view.

One does find passages in the Bible that infer the destruction of the Earth. One example states, "Heaven and Earth will pass away but the word of the Lord will endure forever" (Matthew 24:35). But other than these words serving as expressions of warning against any kind of idolatry, why would Jesus promise "the meek shall inherit the Earth," only to obliterate it?

called to live in, what Lewis calls Narnia, is not a different world somewhere else, but the same world, only lived more deeply, "a deeper country. Every rock and flower and blade of grass as if it meant more."[94] The Creator is on the side of fullness of life, and is even working to heal the wounds of Cain's rebellion. God is calling all Taker cultures back to the community of life.

Is there hope?

I heard Holocaust survivor and Nobel Peace Prize recipient Elie Weisel speak at the University of Arizona in 2005. At one point he described the feeling of powerlessness in the face of evil, and his antidote. I don't have the exact quote, but I remember words to this effect: "I speak out to change the world, but also to keep the world from changing me." Perhaps more and more people are hearing that message and showing courage.

Is there hope?

In March 2008, even the conservative Southern Baptist Convention, currently the largest Protestant group in the United States with 16.3 million members, implemented "A Southern Baptist Declaration on the Environment and Climate Change." In it they declared that their denomination has been "too timid" in the care of God's creation. Members of the convention affirmed that "the current evidence for global warming is substantial, and the threat too grave to wait for perfect knowledge."[95] Perhaps they and other religious groups will find ways to end their historical sanctioning of and participation in (and obvious financial beholding to) Cain's Taker ways.

Is there hope?

Family systems theory teaches that all systems in the plasma of life seek homeostasis. This is true of relationships, families, communities, and the wider ecosystem. God has put natural forces of resilience into the evolving community of life, which are working hard to counter Cain. Perhaps these forces

---

94. Barbara Rossing, *The Rapture Exposed: The Message of Hope in the Book of Revelation*, 8.

95. Rachel Zoll, *S. Baptists: Environmentalism is Biblical Duty*, The Associated Press, 10 March 2008.

will succeed.

Is there hope?

Charles L. Campbell, in *The Word Before the Powers: An Ethic of Preaching*, speaks of a small village in southern France called Le Chambon sur Lignon (population 5,000), whose residents saved approximately 5,000 Jewish men, women and children from the German death camps during the Nazi years. They did it by displaying ordinary courage. They were not super wealthy, super righteous, super religious, super intelligent, or super heroes. They were normal people acting with ordinary courage. Perhaps ordinary people will meet today's challenges.[96]

Is there hope?

Kathleen Billman and Daniel Migliore, in *Rachel's Cry: Prayer of Lament and Rebirth of Hope*, offer an important distinction between hope borne in lament and responses like resignation, presumption, or illusion. They write:

> Resignation is accepting the way things are without complaint or resistance. It is, in effect, saying, "This is the way things are. They will never be different. I must simply accept the way the world is with all its suffering and injustice." Lament refuses to make this concession.[97]

Perhaps enough people will begin to lament and cry out in resistance against the course we are on. Or, having experienced the shivering darkness of beginning disasters first hand, they will say, "No more!"

Is there hope?

Brian McLaren envisions an emerging and growing "community of people who begin to wake up to the covert curriculum in which they swim each day" and once again become resisters like "Jesus' original band of disciples," who perceive that "another

---

96. Charles L. Campbell, *The Word Before the Powers: An Ethic of Preaching*, 1–3, 93, 181.

97. Kathleen D. Billman and Daniel L. Migliore, *Rachel's Cry: Prayer of Lament and Rebirth of Hope*, 125.

world is possible, available for all who believe."[98] Abel holds out the aching hope that the meek will indeed inherit the Earth, which will be immeasurably better not just for humanity, but for the whole.

---

98. Brian McLaren, *Everything Must Change: Jesus, Global Crisis, and a Revolution of Hope*, 292.

Chapter 12
Yes, a Little

Is there hope? The answer is yes, a little. At least enough for me to want to write this book and, along with others, try to be an agent of change. But it will take a hefty dose of fortitude emboldened and empowered by God's gritty grace and interminable forbearance.

It is important to note that though Cain's story dominates the air we breathe (and airwaves we listen to), it is not humanity's story. This is good news. It is not even Earth's story, nor God's story. This is even better news. Rather, Cain's story is a recent glitch. It is the story of only one human culture or group out of thousands and thousands that have lived in God's garden throughout the generations. So to discard it is not to discard something essential to our humanity.

Is there hope? At least three possibilities beckon from the future:

1. **The cancer may kill the body.** This is a terrifying prospect, but describes the current course.

2. **The cancer may one day run its course and become benign.** This is a good news-bad news state of affairs. Yes, the cancer may stand down. Yes, it may lose steam. But the damage done in the meanwhile is and will be a great and terrible waste. However, in his book *Beyond Civilization: Humanity's Next Great Adventure,* Daniel Quinn describes several "civilizations" of humans who walked away from the Taker lifestyle. Why? Because they realized its futility. And there are people today, some of them Christians, trying to leave Takerism and find a better way. They see where it is headed and don't want to lose their spirit, their souls. Though Cain's motto is "persevere, even to extinction," humans can and do sometimes walk away.

   Think about technology, for example. Cain embraces it with considerable loyalty and worries tremendously about keeping up. Universities, corporations, churches, and households have invested much of their philosophical underpinnings and material resources in the direction of technology. They see it as the backbone of modern life and wave of the future. But consider these paradoxes: because of technology, humans currently have access to more bytes of information than ever before (via twenty-four-hour news channels, the Internet, etc.). But are we really more *informed*? And although the volume of new knowledge multiplies daily, is this necessarily translating into increased *wisdom* among our species? And finally, while the *communications* industry has exploded beyond our wildest imaginations over the past fifty years (with the Internet, iPhones, Facebook, Twitter, etc.), one has to wonder whether real *communication*—with our neighbors, our enemies, the garden, between generations and cultures, with strangers, and even with our Creator— isn't just as difficult as it ever has been. In fact, maybe we have even regressed. So my question is this: why are we allowing the relentless pursuit of more and more thingamajigs, thingamabobs, doohickies, widgets, dotcommers, e-learners, and doodads be the leading edge in defining our humanity and guiding our destiny?[99]

3. **The cancer may repent and respond to God and the garden's healing.** For this third possibility to occur, new programs will not do the job. Daniel Quinn is right; we don't need more programs and agencies. This will merely rearrange the furniture as we try still to make something good out of a sinking myth. Rather, we need a better narrative, one that does not position *Homo sapiens* apart from God's creative adventure. We need a narrative that includes humans in the midst of life along with bacteria, hummingbirds, Alaskan elk, ocean coral reefs, subatomic particles, melting glaciers, Harris hawks, river deltas, and Wisconsin apple trees.

---

99. I chuckled and groaned at two stories reported on the radio in 2008. One told of middle school students holding parties where they all sit in a room and "text" each other, that is, communicate electronically instead of in person. Another described "silent rave" dances. College students come together to dance. However, the rooms are mostly silent. No loud bands, little conversation. Each person is plugged into the earphones of their own iPods, listening and dancing to their own private bands and songs. If these stories are just fun theme parties that people try for the fun of it, well, no problem. But if these are metaphors for our culture, we're in trouble!

Chapter 13
Finding Abel

What will need to happen for this to become reality? What needs to be accomplished for Cain's story to lose its momentum, find its demise, and slip into the museums of history? And what needs to be done for Abel's story to emerge from the forgotten corners of God's garden to transform the 6.6 billion (in 2010) members of *Homo sapiens*, for the sake of God's beloved whole community of life?

The solution will require us to begin raising Abel, rather than continue raising Cain. It will call for wisdom more than intelligence, artificial or otherwise, which is a tall order. That is why the response to the question "Is there hope?" is yes, a little.

Such a statement of faith, or lack thereof, may very well be apostasy for a person who claims to be Christian. Our community speaks hope-filled words, such as the following:

- "Even though I walk through the valley of the shadow of death [which may describe our current or near future predicament] I will fear no evil, for you are with me" (Psalm 23:4).

- "So shall my word be that goes forth from my mouth; it shall not return to me empty, but it shall accomplish that which I purpose, and succeed in the thing for which I sent it" (Isaiah 55:11).

- "With humans it is impossible, but nothing will be impossible with God" (Luke 18:26).

- "God was in Christ reconciling the world to himself, not counting their trespasses against them" (2 Corinthians 5:19).

- "My grace is sufficient for you, for power is made perfect in weakness" (2 Corinthians 12:9).

- "Let us not grow weary in doing what is right, for we will reap at harvest time, if we do not give up. So then, whenever we have an opportunity, let us work for the good of all" (Galatians 6:9–10a).

- "I can do all things through Christ who strengthens me" (Philippians 4:13).

Also consider these words:

- "If you truly amend your ways and your doings, if you truly act justly one with another, if you do not oppress the alien, the orphan, and the widow, or shed innocent blood in this place, and if you do not go after other gods to your own hurt, then I will dwell with you in this place, in the land that I gave of old to your ancestors forever and ever" (Jeremiah 7:5–7).

- "God chose what is foolish in the world to shame the wise; God chose what is weak in the world to shame the strong; God chose what is low and despised in the world, things that are not, to reduce to nothing things that are" (1 Corinthians 1:27–28).

- "For freedom Christ has set us free. Stand firm, therefore, and do not submit again to the yoke of slavery" (Galatians 5:1).

- "Now is the acceptable time, see, now is the day of salvation" (2 Corinthians 6:2b).

And consider this countercultural promise for a better day:

- "Blessed are the meek, for they will inherit the Earth" (Matthew 5:5).

These are hopeful words from the Hebrew and Christian scriptures articulating well the heart of God. But the challenges at this late date are still daunting and worthy of the prayer "I believe; help my unbelief."

Yet, we move forward. What needs to be done?

Citizens will need to reclaim our educational systems from teaching, promoting, and trying to equip students for a life of success in Takerism. Colleges and universities are especially pivotal in this regard. They wield substantial influence in shaping how we think about God's garden and humanity's purpose. Consider even these few areas of study, as well as the very important consulting work professors and researchers in these disciplines do in the community:

industrial agribusiness	animal sciences
microbiology	material sciences
architecture	childhood development
education	accounting
criminal justice	aerospace engineering
marketing	civil engineering
optical sciences	hydrology
theater arts	African studies

American history	religious studies
linguistics	cognitive science
physiology	nursing
pharmacy	public health administration
astronomy	ecology
evolutionary biology	mathematics
law	molecular and cellular biology
anthropology	palaeoanthropology
speech and hearing sciences	physics
geology	political science
philosophy	sociology
journalism	business management
psychology	communications

What if powerhouse undergraduate and graduate departments teaching in these areas were to become laboratories of Abel's anthropology, worldview, and theology rather than Cain's? Not by sequestering Abel to the past in esoteric publications and museums. Not by honoring Abel with displays of quaint cultural traditions, ceremonies, costumes, or holidays. But by investing our brightest and best in learning how to live Abel's sustainable way for today and into the future.[100]

Further, humans who find meaning in religious practices and traditions, including Christianity, will need to reclaim their faiths from Takerism. As a Christian, I find it humbling to think that my community by and large has not kept our hands off God's Tree. We wage war against the community of life. We have been instruments in killing. We regress into silence or patriotism in Cain's nonstop scramble to protect the prerogatives of

---

100. Cain likes to acknowledge Abel, but only as a relic from the past or as a current but cryptic oddity on a remote Pacific island somewhere. Perhaps it's similar to the way Martin Luther King Jr. has been turned into a holiday, that is, someone to celebrate, but not to learn from sufficiently to emulate. It's a similar situation with Jesus of Nazareth. Many Cains lift up Jesus' name at every opportunity with boisterous hosannas and shouts of bold acclamation, but then go on to live private, cultural, and national lives fundamentally at odds with Jesus' Abel living.

overconsumption. These are generalizations, certainly. Occasional Abel living can be found in the Christian community and other religions. There is generosity of spirit and money, as well as examples of inspiring service and sacrificial benevolence. There are noble charities and people who give up their lives to subvert injustice. There are hospitals and nursing homes, food banks and thrift stores, schools and shelters. The accumulated efforts are in some ways remarkable.

But Abel is losing the battle. That is the indictment of our time. And increased programming won't change the course, because it's the *story* that is amiss.

Further, humans will need to reclaim the political process from facilitating Takerism. Notice how Cain even distracts us from the genius of democracy by getting the public focused on elections and politics. The race and political battle becomes all consuming—polls, missteps and misspeaks, charges and countercharges, and the ins and outs of voting machines or roll calls. It's high drama, thrills and spills, another opportunity for Wolf Blitzer (of CNN) and others to hyperventilate. But the true test of leadership in a democracy lies in how it behaves *between* elections. Does it address issues honestly? Is it democratic? Does it represent the variety of viewpoints of substance within a diverse population? Or does it virtually shut out and shut down the other 48 percent who did not vote a certain way, let alone the 50 percent of eligible voters who couldn't bring themselves to support either candidate or bill. Tyrants get votes. Dictators win elections. That's the relatively easy part. The real and more difficult test is whether governing serves the community of life between elections. Cain assumes that winning an election is a mandate for winner-take-all behavior until the next vote.

Members of *Homo sapiens* will need to once again take up their roles as part of a pioneer species in Earth's story of life. We must relearn from the millions of years of accumulated wisdom in the garden, rather than look for redemption in technology. Technology has become the false god of the twentieth and twenty-first centuries. It is our "ultimate concern," a phrase used by theologian Paul Tillich. We turn to it for inspiration, solace, even blindness. (A true God doesn't want anyone to follow blindly. Only false gods require that.) Technology has a way of compartmentalizing daily living. It treats the garden as if it were a commodity. It treats humans and other creatures as objects. So again, why have we allowed this portion of life to be the leading edge of what defines true living?

Understand that this is not to say all technology is Takerism. Certainly, technology in line with God's ethical foundations in the garden is a blessing.

In short, humanity will need to learn how to live again.[101] We will need to let loose the massive storehouse of intellect, financial capital, energy, and endowments that are currently dedicated to furthering Cain's folly, and redirect these resources to benefit, or keep from harming, the wider family. We will need to dedicate ourselves to denouncing Cain's claim to be the end (goal) of creation, so that members of *Homo sapiens* no longer enact a story that will see to it that our species indeed is the end of creation. While Cain's story sees a future of a few generations at best, Abel's has considerable hopefulness.

Certainly, we will require effective leadership to do this. But can we rise to the task? If effective leadership skills has been so successful in achieving Cain's goals, why shouldn't such

---

101. Two small-scale examples: (1) While away, a bird's nest with two eggs appeared on the wreath hanging on our front door. We decided to use the back door for a couple of months. (2) Last spring our house showed beginning evidence of termites near the bottom of one wall in the garage. It took five minutes to remove the six termite "tunnels," and one minute to spray a little bug killer on the tunnel spots. We then called an exterminator. They recommended digging conduits under the whole foundation of our house, and regularly dispersing insecticides in them. They also wanted to release these chemicals ten feet into the yard all around the house—to eliminate (annihilate) any possibility of threat. This service would cost $700 for two years. We declined the offer. Termites don't have a right to overrun us, and we don't have a right to overrun termites (and fumigate other life). We can live together. To date, the termite tunnels have not returned, and the rest of the house is termite free.

skills be just as successful in achieving Abel's? However, having said this, I also wonder if this might be naive. While the goal is possible, it is also true that Cain's ways are easier to accomplish. Marketing warfare is always easier than waging relationship, de-evolving into violence is always easier than choosing nonviolent but assertive resistance. Polluting is easier than taking responsibility, getting knowledge easier than gaining wisdom, disliking easier than having compassion, hoarding easier than taking what is necessary and leaving the rest. However, it may also be true that Cain is working harder and longer today to achieve and maintain his destruction than Abel ever had to work in human history (and without the hypertension, ulcers, cancer, and crime).

But mostly, honesty will be required—of ourselves as a species, with God, and with the garden. Those opposed to God's ways develop schemes to obfuscate the shadow side of their actions. They do not want their deeds exposed. They operate behind closed doors as secrecy becomes the operant motif of the day and transparency withers. A kind of narcoticized insensibility to reality settles in. Even Jesus mentions that those who do evil do not seek the light. Cain wants this for his subjects and uses much of the news media, government, commercialism, and some forms of entertainment to achieve it. In contrast, Abel's way prefers truth.[102]

In the middle of revisions for this book, my wife alerted me to another of Michael Pollan's books titled *In Defense of Food*. His opening line brilliantly sums up the Abel way of life regarding responsible eating and health: "Eat food. Not too much. Mostly plants."[103] There you have it: the formula for sustainable living.

---

102. Jesus said, "Everyone who is doing evil hates the light, and does not come to the light, lest their deeds be exposed" (John 3:20). Similarly, "we don't do body counts" is not only a successful strategy for furthering Cain's warfare strategies against humans, along with Orwellian terms like "target" and "collateral damage" in speaking about life, it is also a strategy for the ongoing warfare against God's garden. The true consequences of our actions are hidden in plain sight unless we have eyes to see and ears to hear.

103. Michael Pollan, *In Defense of Food*, 1.

The only thing I would add is regular exercise. Such simplicity and wisdom. Right?

Well, such common sense would probably shake the foundations of Cain's world. "Eat food" would render obsolete "food-like" substances. Food-like substances, i.e., processed foods and imitations, require, create, and bankroll multibillion-dollar industries that span the globe. The research, development, production, promotion, and distribution of these substances— often injected with cheap calories of sugar and fat, with fake sweeteners and artificial flavorings that lie to our senses, and with concocted "nutrients" of dubious value—is a worldwide corporate industry. Paul Roberts in his monumental food systems analysis book, *The End of Food,* even argues that because the industrial food industry can't really survive on a mere 1 percent annual growth in population (Wall Street investors are not satisfied with a 1 percent return on their investments), they must find ways to get people to eat larger quantities.[104] Processed food is the best vehicle for that endeavor. So people working in those industries would have to find jobs that are more wholesome if we were to take Pollan's advice.

Further, eating "not too much" would render obsolete over-indulging. If people ate real food, they would likely eat less, because their bodies wouldn't be starved for real nutrition. This would result in less food needing to be produced, marketed, sold, and shipped. It would require fewer companies, employing less people. Much of the pharmaceutical and diet book industries, which thrive on the diseases that go with eating too much— heart disease, diabetes, stroke, cancer, asthma, esophagus problems, obesity—would have less to do, too.

And eating "mostly plants" would reduce the demand for meat (notice that this doesn't mean no meat, just less), as well as processed and imitation foods. Food would again be grown mostly locally and would have to be complementary to what is sustainable in that locale. This would affect the shipping

---

104. Paul Roberts, *The End of Food*, chapter 4.

and trucking industries, too, which depend on people in Ohio buying head lettuce from farmers in California, and farmers in Nebraska getting livestock feed from producers in Argentina.

Modern food production costs are surprisingly high, according to Richard Heinberg, especially in terms of fossil fuels. He writes:

> Modern industrial agriculture has become energy-intensive in every respect. Tractors and other farm machinery burn diesel fuel or gasoline; nitrogen fertilizers are produced from natural gas; pesticides and herbicides are synthesized from oil; seeds, chemicals, and crops are transported long distances by truck; and foods are often cooked with natural gas and packaged in oil-derived plastics before reaching the consumer. If food-production efficiency is measured by the ratio between the amount of energy input required to produce a given amount of food and the energy contained in that food, then industrial agriculture is by far the least efficient form of food production ever practiced.[105]

The bottom line is that a Michael Pollan version of Abel's way of life would render superfluous many of Cain's ambulance-chaser industries: the nutritional-experts industry, the massive food-marketing and coupon industry that tries to get us to buy processed specimens and eat lots of them, and some journalism. Michael Pollan, himself a journalist, writes how his industry thrives on the confusion accompanying the endless and mostly contradictory food nutrition studies that come out every few months. It is big business, and surprisingly is mostly hocus-pocus.

To Cain's way of thinking, all this sounds like wild and crazy idealism. It seems naive at best, if not downright dangerous. Here is where Cain will want to talk about the real world and human nature in ways that allow his agendas to endure. His thinking has become so clouded that it is hard for him to see.

---

105. Richard Heinberg, *The Party's Over: Oil, War, and the Fate of Industrial Societies*, 193.

But members of *Homo sapiens* should know what the wider community of life, the Creator, and Abel cultures all know, that is, that such wild and crazy idealism is not only doable, it is common sense. Cain's story is really the naive and dangerous thing. Simply put, it is ruinous.

In part IV, we explored hopefulness. Will it be possible or likely that Cain can repent, lay down his arms, and find amendment of life? Can Abel find the means not only to reclaim educational systems, governments, the news media, the military, business, and the food industry from Takerism, but can he also reclaim Christianity and other religions from Takerism?[106] Can there be a national movement? Can there be an international change of heart?[107] Are there already Abel nations lying in wait, or in the making, or segments of Abel cultures living in the midst of Cain cultures, that can step up and fill the leadership void?

Though Cain will insistently fight on as he has in the past, and though the evidence gives plenty of reason to be downcast, there is reason to be mildly hopeful. Not optimistic. Not sanguine. Not Pollyanna. Not even "positive thinking." Just hopeful.

We can be hopeful because humanity itself is not fatally flawed, though it is quite ill, which ironically makes healing a possibility. And we can find hope in the belief that despite the terrors committed in the past 6,000 to 10,000 years, terrors that

---

106. I am focusing mostly on the Christian faith in this book because that is what I know best and am trying to live. I am unqualified to speak of other religions because I understand them only in theory, and haven't taken the time to know them intimately and practice them.

107. It is sobering to observe both China and India (representing 37 percent of Earth's human population) taking up the challenge to consume and pollute like the United States and other wealthy nations. Unfortunately, decades of failed leadership on our part has earned us marginal moral sway on the global stage. We have squandered much.

are now overtly apparent and escalating in our day, God has yet to give up on us. And we can find hope in knowing that indeed this is God's world, and God has a stake in saving it.

So perhaps a better answer to the question, Is there hope? is, "Yes, but probably not in the short term." In other words, the Creator will see to it that the gift of life will endure ultimately, as all creation moves toward greater and greater interrelatedness, diversity, sustainability, and meaning. But for the next 50 to 100 years, the community of life, including humans, will suffer the consequences of Cain's several-thousand-year ill-fated attempt to reign. Freshwater supplies will dwindle, sea life will founder, economies will deteriorate, energy availability will decrease, and wars will metastasize perhaps to the point of atomic bomb madness. The stress of Cain's folly will increase physical, emotional, and social sickness. A monster has been created with no rapid remedy. Again, as the saying goes, "If it's 100 miles into the woods, it's 100 miles out of the woods."

Some will wish for a miracle. Some will pray for a divine quick fix that spares Earth, including *Homo sapiens,* from the consequences of Cain's sin. However, true healing doesn't occur with the addict's desired quick fix. Rather, true healing requires a long-term process utilizing the plethora of tools available: intervention, surgery, wound management, rigorous therapy, tough love, time, forgiveness, medicine, reality checks, encouragement, prayer, amendment of life, prioritization, and especially relationship. A friend who spent time in Tanzania, a country with roots in Abel living, reports that when a person is ill and sees a physician for medical care, the first question the doctor asks is, "What relationship in your life is broken?" Tanzanian culture understands that illness is fundamentally relationship based. What is strained between me and my neighbor, my family, the wider community of life, God, and my own inner soul, works to compromise my immune systems and gets played out in the physical and emotional infirmities that arise in my life.

What gives me hope for the long term is an underlying trust in the Creator's profound goodness, which includes the

Creator's providence for implanting resilience into the creation itself. The Earth will eventually heal, marginalize, or spit out Cain's culture. The hardened ground will eventually crack, and new growth will break through. I'm arguing that a new narrative is a crucial part of that process. In fact, I'm arguing that without this new narrative, most of humanity, including Christians, will continue to be on the wrong side of God's story.

In part V we will examine what a reconsidered and newly framed Christian story might look like.

Part Five
Reframing the Christian Story

Chapter 14
Why Jesus?

So where does Jesus fit in? What does all this mean for the Christian faith, for the church, for Christians?

For many, these questions are irrelevant. For them, Christians are hopelessly under the spell of Cain and are far more the problem than the solution. While I agree with much of this conclusion, I'm also suggesting that it's time for a reconsideration. Christians need to take another look at our own story which has grown small, and find God's larger narrative. And perhaps the rest of the world might benefit from taking another look at a reframed Christian story, too.

If our universe has been around for 13.7 billion years,[108] Earth for 4.6 billion, single-cell life on Earth for 3.7 billion, multi-cellular life for between 1.2 billion and 660 million, trilobites and brachiopods and cephalopods and vibrant reef systems for 425 million, land life for 395 million, reptiles for 295 million (including dinosaurs up until 65 million years ago), mammals (with warm blood, spines, and hair) for 210 million, primates for 20 million, predecessor hominid species for 3 to 4 million, fire use for 800,000, *Homo sapiens* for 200,000 years, modern *Homo sapiens* for 70,000 years, and Cain's culture for the past 6,000 to 10,000 years, here is the million-dollar question: why did the roots of Judaism and Christianity itself emerge only 4,000 and 2,000 years ago, respectively? (To help keep these and other datings straight, see Figure 1 on page 104.)

As a Christian, this seems odd to me. I wonder how God had been relating to the community of life for all those eons and eras, including 200,000 years with *Homo sapiens* prior to these new religions. I wonder why God saw the need to reveal these

---

108. A light beam travels at the speed of 186,000 miles per second in a vacuum (or 670 million miles per hour). Light radiating from our sun takes eight minutes to reach Earth. Light traveling from the nearest star (besides our sun) to Earth, Proxima Centauri, takes 4.2 years to reach us. Light coming from the nearest galaxy, Andromeda, takes 2.5 million years. Hence, we have no idea what the Andromeda Galaxy looks like today, only what it looked like 2.5 million years ago. Along these lines, in March 2008, the astronomy world experienced a thrill. An exploding gamma ray of light, which had burst from an aging star 7.5 billion light-years away (light travels 5.87 trillion miles in 1 Julian year, i.e., every 365.25 days), finally reached the Earth. Astronomers could see back in time. They could see an image of light that had begun traveling to Earth 7.5 billion years ago. See article by Seth Borenstein of the Associated Press, entitled "Huge Star Burst was Halfway Across Universe" in the *Arizona Daily Star* (March 22, 2008): A13.

faiths so late in the game. And why to human beings?[109] Was it because we were so exceptional, or because we were the one species who for all our potential had strayed so dangerously off course? Was it because God's evolutionary pioneer had mistakenly bought into one of the more aberrant cultures of its own species and become disconnected from the Tree of Life? After only a few thousand years of the spreading Cain insurgence, perhaps the Creator was hearing the blood of Abel crying out from the ground. Perhaps God was also hearing the cries of the wider community of life as it was beginning to bear the brunt of Cain's homicidal and suicidal behavior. Even though the full extent of Cain's destruction wouldn't become fully obvious for centuries, was God acting to ward off disaster? I suggest that God addressed our species so late in the game to announce the reign of God in the forms of Judaism and Christianity (and perhaps other religions, too), not because humans were so exceptionally special or superior, but because we were becoming so exceptionally dangerous. As Jesus said, "The son of man came to seek out and to save the lost" (Luke 19:10).

The traditional framing of the Christian story usually goes like this: there's prehistory, and then there is history. During prehistory, humans lived vacant, lost lives. For some reason, God didn't have much to do with them, so they just wandered around in an aimless state of corruption and indifference.

---

109. "Reveal." I understand how psychological and sociological forces shape the development of religious faith. Also, I agree that much in the Hebrew and Christian scriptures is a product of human thinking as people tried to describe perceived experiences with the divine. Even decisions about which individual biblical books were ultimately included or left out were the result of inspired and uninspired human politics, intrigue, and just plain old voting. So a majority vote in formulating the scriptural canon doesn't guarantee a discernment of the will of God any more than does a majority vote in a presidential election.

However, I also don't believe religion or the Bible is solely a product of human inspiration or fabrication. I want to be clear that I am indeed embracing a view that there is a Creator God, who intersects and interacts with Creation. This Creator God in some ways even inspired human writers of the Bible (see more in appendix A, *Biblical Interpretation*).

According to this traditional framing, at one point in the prehistory story, God made an attempt to remedy the situation by flooding the whole Earth. The Creator murdered all creatures except aquatic life, all members of *Homo sapiens* except one small clan belonging to Noah and his wife, and all land species except one male and one female of each land species.[110] After this mythical debacle, God promised never to do such a thing again. Perhaps this change of heart was because human wickedness started up in Noah and his household almost immediately. So much for wiping out bad people to solve problems!

On another occasion in the storytelling, when people came up with the notion of building skyscrapers of hubris to reach into the heavens "and make a name for ourselves," God dispersed all of humanity and jumbled their languages (Genesis 11:1–11).

Then history began (as recounted in Genesis chapter 12 and onward). The Lord tried other methods to heal this wayward species. God fashioned a chosen people whose righteous living would show the rest of humankind how to live, as summarized by the prophet known by scholars as First Isaiah:

> It shall come to pass in the latter days that the mountain of the house of the LORD shall be established as the highest of the mountains, and shall be raised above the hills; all the nations shall flow to it, and many peoples shall come and say, 'Come, let us go up to the mountain of the LORD, to the house of the God of Jacob; that he may teach us his ways and that we may walk in his paths.' He shall judge between the nations, and shall decide for many peoples; and they shall beat their swords into plowshares, and their spears into pruning hooks; nation shall not lift up sword against nation, neither shall they learn war any more (Isaiah 2:2–4; similar

---

110. Actually, while the narrative in Genesis 6:19 and 7:8–9 reports one pair of each animal brought unto the Ark, in contrast, Genesis 7:1–5 reports seven pairs of clean animals and one pair of unclean animals. There is no mention of vegetation. Biblical scholars understand that these two sections were written by several different writers at different times and were blended later by a scribe, or school of scribes.

words are also found in Micah 4:1-4).

However, too often this unique chosenness regressed into notions of special status rather than special service, and the people became models of how not to live. Along with that, God also tried using covenant law to heal people. But while covenant law is necessary, it has limitations. For example, a person can act obediently on the outside but maintain corruption on the inside.[111] Then, God sent kings (presidents, tsars, generals) to lead citizens, only to see them corrupted all too easily. Subsequently God sent prophets to "scare the hell" out of kings and citizens. However, while people cleaned up their act in the face of these scare tactics, dishonesty followed as soon as the heat was off.

Finally, at the right time, after several thousands of years of trying to heal humanity, God came directly. But because God was so awesome, and the overwhelming presence of this power and divinity would cause coronaries in any creature encountered, God "emptied self, taking the form of a slave, being born in human likeness. And being found in human form, he [Jesus] humbled himself and became obedient to the point of death—even death on a cross" (Philippians 2:7–8). This Jesus of Nazareth lived and taught and performed miracles and exorcisms.

But humanity rejected and crucified him, as the story goes. The crucifixion event provided a transformative moment that

---

111. Consider this parable. Once there was a family with three children. Needing to do some errands one day, the parents left the kids at home alone with the following instructions: "Whatever you do, don't put a penny up your nose!" When the parents returned, sure enough, one child had a penny up her nose. The second child had a nickel up his nose, protesting, "You just said not a penny." And the third felt smug. Moral of the story: rules and regulations, the thou shalts and thou shalt nots of life, often brings out the worst in us.

Having told this well-used parable, I also want to confess a tendency among Christians to misrepresent Judaism, sometimes equating it with mindless legalism. Jewish scholar and author Amy-Jill Levine teaches New Testament studies at Vanderbilt University Divinity School. Her recent publications, *The Misunderstood Jew: The Church and the Scandal of the Jewish Jesus*, and an edited collection titled *The Historical Jesus in Context*, have much to teach us Christians about Judaism.

made salvation possible for fallen human beings. The only condition was belief that Jesus died for them, though some added certain greater or lesser behavioral requirements.

Along with the subsequent resurrection, this cross event became the pivotal atonement moment in the history of the world, according to the traditional framing. Everyone who believes in what Jesus did on the cross becomes a recipient of the benefits of that atonement. The temporal Earth passes away, but individuals can be saved now and for eternity in heaven by this atonement. And for those who choose not to believe, God will dispense divine justice and holy rejection in a place of torture for eternity called hell. (Can you imagine a parent, spouse, or friend behaving this way, or saying in other words, "Love me, or I will abuse you forever?")

This is a general rendering of the traditional Christian story. Daniel Quinn insightfully writes about "being saved" this way:

> According to [Cain's] worldview, the human condition is such that everyone is born in an unsaved state and remains unsaved until the requisite ritual or inner action is performed, and all who die in this state either lose their chance for eternal happiness with God or fail to escape the weary cycle of death and rebirth.
>
> Because we've been schooled from birth to understand all this, we're not at all puzzled to hear someone say, "Let me show you how to be saved." Salvation is as plain and ordinary to us as sunrise or rainfall. But now try to imagine how these words would be received in a culture that had no notion that people were born in an unsaved state, that had no notion that people need to be saved. A statement like this, which seems plain and ordinary to us, would be completely meaningless and incomprehensible to them, in part and in whole. Not a word of it would make sense to them.
>
> Imagine all the work you'd have to do to prepare the people of this culture for your statement. You'd have to persuade them that they (and indeed all humans) are born in

a state in which they require salvation. You'd have to explain to them what being unsaved means—and what being saved means. You'd have to persuade them that achieving salvation is vitally important—indeed the most important thing in the world. You'd have to convince them that you have a method that assures success. You'd have to explain where the method came from and why it works. You'd have to assure them that they can master this method, and that it will work as well for them as it does for you.[112]

Since the theories of the atonement go to the heart of most common understandings of Christianity, we will now explore them. Below is a rendering of their meanings, accompanied by a brief critique. From there I attempt to gently set them aside, and ultimately present a newly framed reconsideration. Here are the theories:

1. **The sacrificial theory of atonement.** This theory positions Jesus as the mother of all sacrifices. This Lamb of God who takes away the sin of the world gave his life as a slaughtered sacrifice to God, so that "once and for all" God's need to be sacrificed to is forever satisfied. Adherents say, "Jesus died for me." What they mean is that God provided a sacrifice (Jesus) to satisfy God's requirement, or desire, to be sacrificed to. Benefits are given to those who believe he did that.

    What's wrong with this doctrine? The notion that God gets a kick out of sacrifices, or even ever needed to be sacrificed to, is at best a Taker interpretation and invention. At worst it is a scheme to try to manipulate God. And of course, Christianity is not the only religion to have succumbed to this notion.

2. **The substitution theory of atonement.** This scenario portrays God as seething over human sin. God's built-up anger must be expelled somewhere, and God's need

---

112. Daniel Quinn, *The Story of B: An Adventure of the Mind and Spirit*, 241–242.

for retribution, or retributive justice, must be satisfied. This requires that human sin be punished. However, in grace God decides not to punish humanity. Instead, God provides a substitute. Jesus of Nazareth becomes that sacrificial lamb upon whom the Deity can vent divine wrath. The venting occurs, Jesus dies, and God feels relief. Now, those who believe in Jesus can get God's anger toward them transferred onto Jesus the scapegoat, sparing them from punishment. Adherents say, "Jesus died for me." What this means is that Jesus gave his life to satisfy not only God's anger, but also God's cosmic demand for retributive justice.[113] Adherents say, "I deserve to be punished for sins committed, but Jesus took the hit for me. If I believe this, I'll be saved. I should be grateful and live a good life and tell others that this is the way to get out of deserved punishment."

What's wrong with this doctrine? It portrays the Deity as unable to control anger. Also, it espouses the notion that God's justice requires punishment. What is paramount in this doctrine is that retribution be exacted, whether onto the guilty party, a bad person who is guilty of a different crime, or even an innocent bystander. God's need for retributive justice must be satisfied. I suggest that this popular understanding of the Christian gospel represents the mind and heart of Cain rather than the mind and heart of the Creator.[114]

---

113. Retributive justice, which can be found in the Bible, is a much different form of justice from the deeper biblical notion (in my view) of distributive justice, which is concerned that all have enough and no one has too much.

114. This also sounds similar to a philosophy known informally as "Texas justice," which goes something like this: a crime has been committed. Someone must pay. Hopefully the person who committed the crime will be found. If not, a substitute will be lynched (or invaded), because someone must pay.

3. **The ransom theory of atonement.** Here, Satan has kidnapped humanity away from God's kingdom. God pays a ransom (Jesus' slaughtered life) to get humanity back. Adherents say, "Jesus died for me." They mean, "I was kidnapped, the kidnapper demanded $1 million in ransom (Jesus' death), God came up with the ransom payment, put it in a briefcase (the grave), and gave it to Satan in exchange for me. I am grateful to be free and will live a grateful life and tell others that God will pay their ransom costs too if they believe in Jesus."

   What's wrong with this doctrine? Doesn't it seem strange that God would pay a Satan figure anything, or that God would engage in this kind of dealmaking?

4. **The super-sufferer theory of atonement.** This theory argues that God was so impressed with the heroic x-rated sufferings of Jesus and the devotion to God such willingness to suffer demonstrated, that God has decided to forgive everyone who believes in this *Braveheart* sufferer. This is the basic theology of Mel Gibson's 2005 film, *The Passion of the Christ.* Adherents say, "Jesus died for me." They mean, "Jesus suffered a lot so I don't have to if I will believe in him. However, I can show my gratitude by enduring the suffering that will likely accompany my following of Jesus."

   What's wrong with this doctrine? Redemptive suffering portrays God as either masochistic or sadistic, depending on how one understands Jesus. It can also glorify unjust suffering, and in a curious way even make war seem noble. On a more individual level, sometimes a wife who is beaten by her husband can even be counseled to "accept this burden" as an honorable and redemptive "cross to bear." Few people today see this as a wise, healthy response, however.

These theories of the atonement permeate much of Christian theology, and certainly the popular religions of Cain's culture. Here is one example. Recently, I tuned into a television rerun of a 1980s Billy Graham crusade. I hadn't listened to this evangelist preach in years, and it brought back memories from childhood. Billy Graham is a respected person and a gifted communicator. He has counseled many people to lead better lives. He speaks of his faith with ease and conviction. However, as I listened to his message, I realized something in me had changed. I realized I didn't believe in what he was saying. If this is Christianity, I said to myself, then I'm not a Christian. Basically the point of the sermon and crusade was this: Christianity is all about the question of who goes to heaven and who goes to hell, and what a person has to do or not do, believe or not believe, in order to get to either place. And by the way, one had better make one's decision pronto because God is about to obliterate the world, and whoever doesn't get right with God and name Jesus as his or her Lord and Savior in time will be excluded from God's loving embrace forever. There are many denominational variations on this theme, but it is a basic theology of many of Cain's religions. And this is the narrative I no longer believe.

But if such traditional theories of the atonement fall short, portraying a terribly diminutive God in my view, what, then, is this Jesus really about? Who is this woodworker from Nazareth? Why did he live? Why then? What significance accompanied the incarnation (enfleshment)? Why did Jesus behave so contrary to his culture? What do his teachings, miracles, and exorcisms accomplish? How does his gruesome crucifixion, startling resurrection, mysterious ascension, and Holy Spirit presence in the world affect the creation today?

Volumes have been written on these questions, but here is my attempt at a response in light of this new framing:

The Jesus event (including Jesus' birth, life as a human, servant ministry, speaking out against injustice, tragic crucifixion, real death, and counterintuitive resurrection) demonstrates in the clearest possible way God's preference for the fragrant offerings of Abel, that is, for Abel's way of Leaver living. It proclaims God's profound desire for wayward humanity to rejoin the community of life so that the world may be saved. Further, it is a harsh reminder that living the Abel way of life will often trigger a violent reaction from Cain. Takers will always fight to destroy Abel, because cancer knows only how to destroy. However, we are not to worry. Even if persecutions come our way, we are not to despair. Why? Because not only is Abel's way filled with honor and goodness, it is also ultimately immune to Cain's final sedition. "Not even death will be able to separate us from the love of God in Christ Jesus our Lord" (Romans 8:38–39).

The cross event then becomes central. The beams of wood bearing a dying Abel of Nazareth stand as *mirror* and *window*. As *mirror*, the wood with Jesus on it reflects back to me the true nature of my Takerism. What does my Takerism look like? It looks like the Creator's goodness in human form and in living color shattered and crucified by me and mine. That's its ugliness. That's the rub. And lest I think my Taker ways are not that big of deal, or that they can be covered up or rationalized away, the cross forces me to encounter sin's display in all its misshapen splendor.[115]

But the cross event is also *window*. Through this window of the outstretched arms of the Abel Christ, all Creation is granted a holy glimpse into the broken heart of God, and into the essence of God's love for the cosmos, including humans, including Abel, and surprisingly including Cain. This love has an immensity of grace that surpasses all understanding. It forgives. It is self-sacrificing. It is expansive, riveting, and life empowering. The cross event boldly proclaims the good news, "God loves this world, including humans, and will not give up on it."

But there is more. There is something even beyond the

---

115. *The Passion of the Christ* movie did an admirable job in showcasing the raw horror of crucifixion. However, it fell short by portraying Jesus' death as unique. Historically, there were hundreds of young Jewish men crucified by Cain's Roman Empire, who similarly and brutally died alone and forsaken.

message of a radical call to Abel living and a privileged peek into the heart of God. That "more" is ontological, I believe. Something happened in this event. Something occurred that transformed reality. The cosmos began to be mended. What happened on Christ's cross was not that the Creator got a holy sacrifice, or that God found a scapegoat on whom to vent divine rage, or that the Deity paid off Satan in exchange for humanity's safe return, or even that the "ground of being" (Paul Tillich's phrase) was moved to mercy by Jesus' willingness to suffer unjustly. Rather, on the Jesus-bearing cross the *powers* of sin and death were overcome. Not sin, but the power of sin. Not natural death, which is part of God's evolving garden of life, but perishing death, which is separation from the community of life, from ourselves, and from God. On this instrument of capital punishment, Jesus dissolved the ultimate hold of sin's power to separate us from the embrace of God. Jesus restored relationship not by means of retaliation, which is Cain's method, and which only plants seeds of counterretaliation and counter-counterretaliation *ad infinitum*, but by embrace. Like a cosmic sponge, Jesus soaked in the horrors of Takerism. He took them into his complete being, body and soul. Fully absorbing them, he let them kill him. Fully forgiving them, he took them with him to the grave. In so doing, he disarmed sin and death's power to cause us to perish. The cross event is the ultimate sign that God's goal is to heal the garden, and that God's means for healing *Homo sapiens* is not life-crushing violence, but life-giving grace.

The following is a strange analogy, but here it goes. When a foreign object invades our body—a thorn, dirt from a scrape, bacteria—white blood corpuscles attack it. They absorb it, devour it, and then commit suicide. Hence, puss, or dead white blood corpuscles. No analogy is complete, but this points in part to what Jesus' death on the cross accomplished. I know this is a faith statement that can't be proven, but in my view, the cross event's meaning is that this special One has absorbed all of Cain's (and Abel's) sin—past, present, and future. That's a lot of sin, and of course, it killed him. Jesus didn't die of an accident, cancer, or even old age. Cause of death? Cain's mutiny (or emancipation, in Cain's eyes). That's what murdered Jesus of Nazareth. That's what ended the life of Mary's son. But at the same time, and again this is my belief, Jesus' death disarmed the power of that foreign object (sin) and destroyed its capacity to truly destroy God's community of life, including humans. All life dies when it is time to get off the stage. As Elizabeth Gray Vining said so well: "Life is a trust, given into our hands, to hold carefully, to use well, to enjoy, to give back when the time comes."[116] Both life and death are intended in God's garden. But this event brought assurance that we would not *perish*, which is a different thing. Again, to perish is to be separated from ourselves, from the Earth, from the community of life, and from God. On the cross, the powers of perishing death were overcome, and the restoration of relationship begun, so that now "neither death, nor life, nor angels, nor rulers, nor things present, nor things to come, nor powers, nor height nor depth, nor anything else in all creation will be able to separate us from the love of God in Christ Jesus our Lord" (Romans 8:38–39).

The cross event is good news—for Abel, for the whole community of life that has suffered so much under Cain's rule, and for Cain. It brings accountability by exposing reality—though God, the garden, and Abel have been seeing reality all along. And through the cross event the Creator meets Cain's terror head-on by establishing a forgiving relationship with such an enemy as this that fears relationship above all else.

One of the most insightful and remarkable books of recent years is *No Future Without Forgiveness,* by Desmond Tutu. In this book, this Anglican bishop and Nobel Peace Prize recipient describes the work of the Truth and Reconciliation Commission (TRC) in South Africa. This commission was established by Nelson Mandela, who, after spending twenty-six years in prison, was elected national president in April of 1994 in the first ever democratic election in that country. I happened to be in Johan-

---

116. As quoted by Roger Prescott in *Day By Day: Seeing the Sacred in Everyday Life*, 194.

nesburg a week before that historic vote and was deeply moved by the courage, spirit of forgiveness, and electric hope stirring among the people.

The premise of the TRC was this: full amnesty would be granted for every crime committed in the name of apartheid. The only condition for receiving such forgiveness was courage. Each state terrorist, that is, each government official who had perpetrated decades of intimidation, harassment, torture, murder, hatred, and lynching upon African families, as well as those African citizens who committed atrocities in the process of trying to fight back, would no longer face indictment, trial, or punishment. They could all receive amnesty full and clear. All they needed to do was come into a courtroom and meet face to face and soul to soul the persons they had formerly harmed. Well, as one can imagine, powerful and emotional moments ensued as perpetrators confessed their own misdeeds of terror in the presence of the very persons, or surviving loved ones, they had robbed of fullness of life. People heard words spoken from wounded souls, felt Earth's presence in fractured lives, and looked into the eyes of traumatized brothers and sisters. People told stories, shed tears, offered forgiveness, received healing, and began reconciliation. Truth telling and humility filled the courtroom chambers as liberation came to many. Again, the only requirement was simple courage. Such a scenario reinforced not only the truth that forgiveness must happen for healing to occur (and that there is no future without forgiveness), but also the truth that forgiveness is never a solo event or one-way street, but a restored relationship.

Of course, sadly, some individuals were unable to find such resolve within themselves and were incapable of reaching out for help. We Cains can be so bound to our Taker worldviews and the notions of superiority and deniability they afford that we will sometimes walk away from the relationship that forgiveness requires. In short, we are not yet able to see the joy of reconciliation. Perhaps like persons diseased with alcoholism, who have a love-hate relationship with this fermented wonder even though it is killing them and those they love, so also some Cains have a love-hate union with their Taker lifestyle, even though it is killing them and the world that God so deeply loves.

Forgiveness requires the courage to begin a connection. Captors will meet captives on equal footing. Fighter pilots operating in fighter planes high in the sky, or in front of remote computer screens thousands of miles away from the people they are sending missiles to kill, will look into the eyes of the women and children and men whose flesh they set ablaze, whose legs they crushed, whose bodies they severed, and whose homes they left in rubble. Polluters (from large corporations to individual persons) will embrace the arms of an aching creation. A soldier will hold close the mother of the daughter or son he killed. Overconsumers will lie down next to the woman who is starving, and the lake that is choking with contamination. And healing will come.

The novel *The Shack*, by William Paul Young, is a moving portrayal of the transformative power of forgiveness in this life, and how forgiveness is a painful but necessary process. I recommend the book. However, for those conflicted relationships now that may not find resolution in this lifetime, I've come to understand heaven as the place of final healing. In other words, I believe that heaven will be open to all. The only requirement will be courage. No instant cures. No rewards. Rather, God will set me down with everyone I have hurt or who has hurt me, including those I love. Now unencumbered, we will have endless time to learn the full weight of one another's stories and being. We will build relationships borne in forgiveness, and forgiveness borne in relationship. It will take work; there'll be no thumb twiddling in the life after our death. But the result of entering this process will be a well being that might well be best described as a feast in paradise. Again, the only condition will be courage.

I once read a story of a twenty-one-year-old college student who had been raped and murdered. The crime was dreadful and the family was devastated. There was the arrest, the trial, the deliberation, the verdict, and the sentencing. On the day of sentencing, the parents requested that the life sentence include an ongoing exchange of letters and visits between them and the prisoner. They wanted the murderer to know them—and their daughter. And they wanted to know her murderer, this man who would forever be part of their lives. The request was made with incredible pain and carried an unbearable weight. But their prayer is that some day the gift of forgiveness and mutual healing may emerge out of this awful bond, engendering a holy release and peace that no amount of revenge or retributive justice could ever impart.

Today, Jesus and his true followers are among those who live out such courage. They are the stewards of God's evolving Tree of Life. They enter into relationship with God, God's garden, Abel, and even Cain. And they nonviolently undermine the cancer at every opportunity, until it repents or becomes benign. They forge a relationship borne in forgiveness, and a forgiveness borne in relationship.

Not surprisingly, passivity is not the way to render Cain benign. Appeasement will only embolden his destructive ways. Rather, Cain must be resisted assertively, boldly, forcefully, and always nonviolently. Nonviolence is imperative. A culture, person, or nation that regresses into the carnage of violence and war as a way to solve problems will always lose its own soul. They will become further cut off from their humanity, and from the community of life. Could it be any more clear than Jesus' own words, namely, "Those who live by the sword, die [internally, if not externally] by the sword" (Matthew 26:52). He spoke these words at a time when violence in his own life could have easily been justified. But bold and assertive nonviolent word-action against the powers and principalities of Cain's kingdom is the only means for true transformation and healing. Unlike war, which destroys, courageous nonviolent resistance generates life.

Having attempted to deconstruct the traditional atonement theories, and even recommended their abandonment, an epilogue of sorts is now perhaps fitting. Something *can* be resurrected, after all. In a sense, Jesus is a sacrifice, in that he lived a self-giving life for others. And certainly "he died for us" in the sense that Jesus died showing us a better way, showing us the heart of God, and by absorbing the corrosive powers of sin and death that will cause us to perish. Indeed, Cain is similar to a kidnapped victim who needs rescuing. And Jesus' suffering connects him to the suffering of a wounded world. Actually, all those destructive atonement theories may be truly life giving when framed in the heart, hands, and worldview of Abel.

Chapter 15
Tools of Resistance and Hope

What tools can we find for Abel living? Tools of resistance, really. If machine guns, missiles, and atomic bombs are not upright for humans, including followers of Jesus Christ, what kinds of weapons of mass construction does the Creator provide? Consider the following passage from Paul's letter to the Ephesians:

> Be strong in the Lord and in the strength of his power. Put on the whole armor of God, so that you may be able to stand against the wiles of the devil. . . . Fasten the belt of truth around your waist, and put on the breastplate of righteousness. As shoes for your feet put on whatever will make you ready to proclaim the gospel of peace. With all of these, take the shield of faith. . . . Take the helmet of salvation, and the sword of the Spirit, which is the word of God (portions of Ephesians 6:10–17).

In Cain's hands, Paul's words seem to normalize personal, tribal, and nationalistic carnage. Indeed, Cain has even engraved crosses on swords and fighter jets. But take a moment to reread the above passage, this time from Abel's perspective. Do you see a difference?

There are other tools of resistance and empowerment, too.

1. **Confession and forgiveness.** Cain's take on Christian faith is flawed because his diagnosis of the problem is flawed. He asserts that the general pathway and story-line of Cain is fine. Yes, we personally screw up once in a while; we gossip, lie a little to get a sale, think too much about sex, or cheat on an exam. Yes, we curse, forget to pray, get angry, or harbor prejudices. There's the divorce, the speeding ticket, the time we didn't go back to the cashier when she undercharged us. So we'll confess these things, be forgiven, and then it's just a matter of standing up and getting back on track again.

   However, in this reconsideration of Christianity, what we are actually owning up to is something more ominous. We are confessing warfare—against God, against Creation, against Abel, and against other Cains. We are confessing mutiny and a willful arrogance (or irresponsible ignorance) that despises the Tree of Life. We are confessing a counterfeit narrative. And because we are addicted to Takerism, we are confessing our very own participation in the powers and principalities of death that stand against God's ways. What we are owning up to is enormous—unforgiveable in fact—all of which makes the gift of forgiveness and reconciliation even more paradoxical, and sweeter.

2. **Baptism and Eucharist as sacraments are also acts of resistance that both God and we participate in.** Cain likes point systems. Cain adores distinctions and classifications, that is, caste systems like those based on wealth, race, creed, military power, neighborhood, affil-

iation, and education. These scoring systems put some above, others even, and most below. The sacraments of baptism and the Lord's Supper together disassemble these ranking schemes and expose their destructiveness. Not only is "there no distinction, since all have sinned and fall short of the glory of God" (Romans 3:22b–23), but "God shows no partiality, but in every nation anyone who fears God and does what is right is acceptable to God" (Acts 10:34–35). To participate in baptism and the Eucharist is to boldly take a stand and declare "No more!" to Cain's worldview and theology, and to be given the strength to live a new way.

3. **Grace is a tool of resistance.** It is sobering to consider that at one point, and probably many times since, God regretted creating a species that could de-evolve into the likes of Cain. In fact, the Genesis writer portrays God as giving consideration to destroying *Homo sapiens* for the sake of a new and better world:

> The LORD was sorry that he had made humankind on the Earth, and it grieved him to his heart. So the LORD said, "I will blot out man whom I have created from the face of the ground, man and beast and creeping things and birds of the air, for I am sorry that I have made them" (Genesis 6:7).

Because of humanity's sin, the writer even scripted the Creator as contemplating the destruction of everything. Such is the gravity and scope of Cain's failure. But God made a decision not to do such a thing (can a mother destroy her children?). The Creator could have taken a hike, gone missing, withdrawn all love and concern, even obliterated everything. But God decided not to. Instead, God put in motion a plan to heal Cain for the sake of all creation.

Though God has revealed this grace through many

Abels down through time—wise ones, leaders, followers, rabbis, prophets, martyrs, neighbors, enemies, children, people within and outside the world's religions—for me, this grace has become most fully demonstrated in and through the life, teachings, practices, counterculture lifestyle, passion, crucifixion, resurrection, and Holy Spirit empowerment of Jesus the Christ. Jesus is God's good news, present and enfleshed. Jesus the Christ is the in-breaking of God's kingdom, reign, and way of living into a Cain-dominated and Cain-broken world. Jesus is God mending the damage, including Cain, for the sake of all creation, including Abel. Jesus is a peek into the heart of God, and into God's future. He is the Creator's forgiving embrace. And in this empowering and Cain-resisting grace, Christians are called to live that future *now* until hopefully and eventually the rest of humanity catches on.

4. **Community also is an important tool of resistance and empowerment for Abel.** Humans need connection: to our inner souls, to other humans, to God, to the evolving Tree of Life. Cain's ways are forever trying to build fences, erect walls, objectify enemies, break apart families, solidify parochialism, hype patriotism, maintain ranking systems, and produce lonely people. Community is taking a stand. It is soul force: an act of nonviolent resistance and reconnection.

    Like many others, I was inspired by the recently revealed diary entries of Mother Theresa of Calcutta. Her raw words startle many people. But there is wisdom in her bared soul. The following are some of the starker and more shocking entries:

    • To a friend she wrote, "Jesus has a very special love for you. As for me, the silence and emptiness is so great that I look and do not see, listen and do not hear. The tongue moves but does not speak."

- "I do not feel God in my heart or in the Eucharist."

- "Lord, my God, you have thrown me away as unwanted, unloved. I call, I cling, I want, and there is no one to answer, no, no one. Alone. Where is my faith? Even deep down right in there is nothing. I have no faith. I dare not utter the words and thoughts that crowd in my heart."

- "I have begun to love my darkness, for I believe now that it is a part, a very small part, of Jesus' own darkness and pain on Earth."

- "I am told God loves me, and yet the reality of the darkness and coldness and emptiness is so great that nothing touches my soul. Did I make a mistake in surrendering blindly to the call of the sacred heart?"

- "The smile is a mask or a cloak that covers everything. I spoke as if my very heart was in love with God, a tender personal love. If you were there you would have said, 'What hypocrisy.'"

- "I feel God does not want me, God is not God, and God does not really exist."

Mother Theresa's experiences are not uncommon, I believe. Such experiences have been my personal and pastoral experience at times as well. But her level of self-honesty is rare. And so refreshing. More than most, she was able to take the blindfolds off as she daily lived and served among the effects of Cain's ways. And it took its toll. Certainly Mother Theresa had deep faith, too. Her diaries and other writings powerfully reveal that side as well. But what strikes me about Mother Theresa's confessions (and this is a reminder for us not to romanticize Abel living, including Abel spirituality, and including Abel Christianity) is that even though she experienced what could be termed a crisis of faith, she persevered in three arenas:

- She fought I-centeredness by continuing to serve.

- She realized that Christianity is not an upwardly mobile religion of self-fulfillment, but a downwardly mobile life of self-emptying service.[117]

- She stayed in community.

Mother Theresa walked the talk. In one apocryphal vignette, she had just spoken at a formal gala to raise money for her work with dying street children in Calcutta. After giving her presentation, while the wealthy benefactors proceeded to dine on their requisite extravagant foods, she slipped into the back kitchen and sat down to a bowl of simple soup.

In another story, a respected journalist came from across the world to interview this legendary Christian woman. After a couple minutes of conversation Mother Theresa announced dryly, "I'm not very interesting." Then, pointing, she quietly invited, "Why don't you talk with that boy in the corner? He'll probably die tonight." Of course her scheme was not to get out of the interview, or even to have the journalist interview the boy. Her aim was more conspiratorial. She wanted this visitor to stay with this child, and maybe even hold him through the night while he died. She wanted his senses, his heart, and his spirit. She wanted to "save" this traveler and help him reconnect with the community of life. Who knows, he might even ask himself, "Why is this boy dying? What is his name? What has been his story? Why do I feel so helpless?" The journalist's life and profession might even begin to be restored—all because of this unforeseen relationship.

---

117. "Downwardly mobile life" is an insight from Shane Claiborne.

The challenges of our time cannot be addressed without finding ways to be more profoundly connected with our human neighbors, and neighbors within the community of life. Somehow, Cain has been able to fashion a culture of deep loneliness. Blogs, Facebook, cell phones, Internet relationships, texting, and chat rooms won't ever be a substitute for real community. And genuine community won't come if we just focus on human relationships either. Community with humans without community with nature or God won't restore Cain's addicted and damaged heart. Sallie McFague expresses this notion nicely when she writes:

> Most Christians either do not know how to relate to nature or they relate to it as Western culture does, as an object for our use. Even notions of stewardship are often couched in the language of conserving resources for future generations— an implicit acknowledgement of its usefulness to human beings. Most Christians draw a line at nature. While God and other people are subjects, nature is not. My suggestion is that we should relate to the entities in nature *in the same basic way* that we are supposed to relate to God and other people—as ends not means, as subjects valuable in themselves, for themselves.[118]

5. **Lament is an act of resistance.** This powerful biblical practice involves seeing and knowing, rather than turning one's eyes or closing one's ears. Lament is opening oneself up to experience. Just as Yahweh heard Abel's blood crying out from the ground (Genesis 4:10), and "observed the affliction of my people who are in Egypt; I have heard their cry on account of their taskmasters. Indeed, I know their sufferings" (Exodus

---

118. Sallie McFague, *Super, Natural Christians: How We Should Love Nature*, 1.

3:7), so, too, are we in our day challenged to hear the whole creation, including Abel, and including Cain, "groaning in travail" (Romans 8:22).

As lament sees, it bears witness. As it hears, it gives acknowledgement and voicing to the pain. The plot line of Daniel Quinn's novel, *Ishmael: An Adventure of the Mind and Spirit,* is basically a gorilla telling a guy what the rest of the community of life thinks about Cain. Through this fictional gorilla character, Quinn is able to give the reader an "other side" perspective, and a new participation in the mounting anguish emanating from Cain's takeover.

And as psalms of lament and books of lament like Lamentations "cry out" from a place of unflinching encounter with unvarnished truth, these lamenters also bear witness to a newfound presence—that of a Creator who "knows," who is already interacting, who is already embracing and mending. In this sacred but ordinary place where reality meets a knowing God, and where suffering is known among the community of life, the one who laments finds empowerment in a relationship with a God who is not forsaking the world to Cain, nor even Cain to himself. God is defeating Takerism so that even the Taker may be healed and welcomed back into the alive garden of normal living and normal dying.

6. **Resurrection is an act of resistance.** On the first Easter, the good news of God was declared from deep within a rock-hewn tomb. How counterintuitive. How revolutionary. Curiously, the ending of Mark's gospel reports that no one said anything to anyone, "for they were afraid" (Mark 16:8). Yet, the word got out. Jesus broke through the deadness of existence back then as he breaks into every moment today bringing all that is truly life giving. Whether into a failure, into the death of a relationship, or into a fire or flood that destroys a

cherished home or city; whether into a heartbreaking rejection, the loss of a job, the mire of an ill-considered war, or declining health; whatever the failure and however the "wolf of insignificance" comes knocking at our doors, sometimes by our own making, sometimes by the misbehavior of others, and sometimes just because we live in an alive garden that includes both life and death, resurrection will always break through to transform the darkest night and mend the most broken of circumstances. New life occurs even today. It comes from God. This is cause for hope.

And when final death comes to each living creature (or as one minister put it, "No one gets out of life alive"), there is hope. This hope is grounded not only in the support and love of the community of life living under the reign of the Creator, but also in the assurance of a new, post-death life of eternity with God and God's community of life in heaven. With such resurrection assurance for both our todays and our tomorrows, followers of Abel of Nazareth will find it hard to cling to a wasteful and wasting, dishonest and dishonorable Taker life now.[119]

---

119. "Afraid to die, we learn to lie" is a line from a Janis Ian song. It captures the corrosive role that the fear of death plays in our lives. To resist succumbing to that fear is a challenge. Yet to cling to the promise of resurrection in this life and after death, is to begin to live well as a member of God's community of life.

As stated several times, in God's garden, mortality is a necessary reality. Everything dies so that others may live. However, with such a 100 percent death rate, it often becomes overwhelming. That's why the Creator and creation itself sews succor, sustenance, and resilience into the fabric of life. There is community, support, prayer, memory, thankfulness, tears, stages of grief and recovery, new life, and the birth of new babies. This resilience is entwined within the very plasma of existence. This is an important part of Jesus' message as I have come to understand it.

Part Six
The Future

So where are we?

On the one hand, the future of the Earth's relationship with most of humankind looks bleak. It is that serious. Cain has mismanaged himself badly. Lord, have mercy. Creation, have mercy. Abel, have mercy. But is it too late for Cain to change? Can the damage be undone? Is there time yet to practice repentance? The present is as good a time as any in which to find out.

Candid confession will be the first important step. A clear-eyed assessment of the scope of our iniquity is the necessary antidote to centuries of denial. Can Takerism do that? It seems possible.

Having admitted our guilt, can God forgive us? This is a huge question. Can the Christian community especially be forgiven by the Creator? For despite claiming to love God, we have been the most irresponsible of all. Yes, God can and will do that.

Can the wider community of life forgive us? Will our own "family of origin" forgive us for disowning and then abusing them? Certainly the community of life can get along fine, or even better given the recent record, without humans. Yet, this community longs to bring one of their own back on board as a reciprocal partner in the evolving Tree of Life.

Can Abel forgive us for what we have done to his ancestors, homelands, languages, and ways of life? Can Abel be healed sufficiently to where he can lead us again into wisdom? Yes, Abel has always understood the union between forgiveness and relationship.

Having met the enemy and discovered the enemy is us, can we forgive ourselves? This may be the most difficult task of all. Can we forgive our own inner Cain soul, our own Cain brothers and sisters, mothers and fathers, and grandmas and grandpas? Can we forgive our recent and revered ancestors who have carried out these awful deeds and taught us to be Takers rather than Leavers? Can we forgive ourselves for our own disregard for those who will come after us? I believe so.

And having received forgiveness from the wronged parties, including ourselves, will we be able to find the courage to live into a restored relationship with God, with creation, with Abel, and with our Cain brothers and sisters? I pray so.

The world belongs to God and God's whole community of life. The notion of human exceptionalism is a false and tragic ideology. The word "idolatry" might even be more appropriate. To live as though there were an ontological gap between *Homo sapiens* and the so-called environment is a scandal. Such a worldview must end. There is *only* the environment, which, it turns out, includes the whole community of life, including *Homo sapiens*. The Creator's goal is simple: that all have enough and no one has too much (2 Corinthians 8:13–15). This will take very great wisdom to grasp, let alone live, but it is our only real choice as the hour grows late.

The good news is that we have the goodwill of the Creator on our side. And we have Abel, especially Abel of Nazareth, on our side. And we have the whole community of life yearning for our maturity. And lest that be insufficient motivation, we also have the voices of coming generations, including our own unborn great-grandchildren and their children, beckoning to us from the future to do the right thing.

In *The Party's Over,* Richard Heinberg devotes the final chapter to describing practicalities for living well.[120] He suggests detailed steps that individual households, communities, nations, and the global village can take. Among other things, he suggests these:

- Individual households can embrace conservation. We can eat organic, natural, and locally grown foods. We can improve energy efficiency. We can learn how to repair things rather than simply discard and buy new (or worse, support an economy that cultivates planned obsolescence).[121]

- Communities can conserve water, promote sustainable and regional agricultural systems, encourage buying local, and fight off "developer" and city government

---

120. Richard Heinberg, 225–262.

121. The CBS program *60 Minutes*, in a segment called "The Wasteland" (produced by Solly Granatstein), reported in August 2009 that U.S. citizens discard 130,000 computers per day (and 100 million cell phones each year). To replace a broken machine is one thing. But to be addicted to faster and faster, more and more, creates uncalled for and preventable electronic trash, or e-waste. The program also examined the recycling industry and found much that was disturbing. Computers and monitors that get turned in for recycling often get sold from one company to another, and then to another, with very little regulation. These machines can end up being dismantled by children in poor nations, with deadly toxins like lead, mercury, chromium, and polyvinyl chlorides spilling into the soils and water systems of their village.

schemes that increase population densities beyond carrying capacity.

- As a nation, we can impede industrial agribusiness, shift the meaning of patriotism away from war glorification to respecting God's garden, invest in policies that promote clean, renewable, and sustainable energy resources, and redefine "national interest" away from Jabba's unruly appetites.

- Globally, the pandemic of human-caused climate change can be addressed cooperatively, with particular sacrifice and newborn responsibility coming from the wealthiest nations.

Many other writers have also described helpful steps to improve the health of the Earth's ecosystem. Inventors, investors, and community leaders need to be turned loose to join Abel's creative energy, sustainable action, and life-preserving values.

However, the core message of this whole book is that unless our cultural and theological narrative is jettisoned, and then replaced, very few of these practicalities will be effective. If we engage in a smattering of ingenious projects and inspired enterprises but keep framing Earth's story, humanity's story, and God's story in the same old way, especially in relation to the notion of human exceptionalism on the one hand, and the presumed advanced status of Cain's way of life on the other, those projects will surely fail. They will morph into Takerism sooner rather than later, and will roar back to bite the community of life with an even greater vengeance and destructiveness. Further, if we continue to enact the Christian story as it has grown small over the centuries, which in my view is the "other gospel" the apostle Paul so strenuously discredited because he anticipated its final depravity, Takerism will persevere. Cain's homicidal/suicidal ways will prevail. Cain's intractable habits will always regress into mindsets such as these:

- Resignation. All is lost.

- Divine Providence. It's in God's hands.

- Denial. What problem?

- Paralysis. It's too overwhelming.

- Muddling through. It's going to be all right, somehow.

- Deflection. It's not my problem.[122]

We are at a crossroads. If this book has merit, it is a shaking of the foundations. I believe this is a good thing.

How one frames a story is not inconsequential. To say that God loves the world, including people, is different than saying God loves people, and also, incidentally, the environment. There are other examples. If one frames the Christian story one way, applying interpretations that emit from that framing and even adding up the number of Bible verses, one can conclude, for example, that *patriarchy* is God's way. However, if framed differently, we can easily see that patriarchy is one of the destructive powers and principalities that God is on a mission to dismantle.

The same is true of the story of Noah and the Flood. In one framing, Yahweh is a god of genocide, so get used to it. But in another, the ultimate message is that if you think killing bad people gets rid of evil, think again. Within days after leaving the Ark, Noah becomes corrupt. He becomes fall-down drunk, projects cursing culpability on his son Ham for witnessing his father's lapse, and condemns Ham's progeny to centuries of enslavement (Genesis 9:18–27).

Or consider the crucifixion and resurrection of Jesus. Or the Pentecost experience. Or the book of Revelation. Or the story of Cain murdering Abel. Even well-known parables such as Jesus' parable of the wedding banquet (Matthew 22:1–14) can take on striking new meanings when framed from Abel's vantage. (See appendix C for a challenging sermon on this text.)

---

122. This list is adapted from a list presented by James Gustave Speth, *The Bridge at the Edge of the World*, 42.

How we frame the story of our own species matters especially. If the Earth is only several thousand years old, and the species *Homo sapiens* appeared right at the beginning, then it might make sense to formulate a worldview with *Homo sapiens* at the center. If, however, we have been around for only the tiniest fraction of time, and have evolved and are evolving just like everyone else, claims of self-importance, or what my colleague Lucas Mix calls "diva theology," may be exaggerated.

This is not to say that every framing has equal validity. There are qualitative differences, as well as strength of argument and factors of evidence and inspiration. But the Christian story of our mother culture's womb is vacant. It has moved the church away from that which is life giving and toward the destruction of the creation (the "cosmos" in the ancient Greek language of John 3:16) that God so loves. To simply live out this traditional version of the Christian story more effectively is not the answer. It will not turn the tide. It has no "horse" for the ordeals facing us.

In Greek thought, there are two words for two kinds of time, *chronos* and *kairos*. *Chronos* is chronological time, by the clock, marking minutes and hours and years. *Kairos* is God's time, in the fullness of the moment. In *chronos* mode, I eat lunch at noon; in *kairos,* I eat when I'm hungry. In *chronos* time, I get married in my twenties; in *kairos,* I marry when I find someone to love with whom I wish to share my life.

Chronos time is running out. Only the largely blind among us do not see this truth.

But God's *kairos* time is not running out. From this deeper reality God's story presses on. In God's *kairos* moments, the community of life will always be sustained and move toward the Creator's purposes. Irrespective of fossil fuel reserves, population growth spurts, and even human mismanagement, God's narrative will endure. *Homo sapiens* may discover alternative energy supplies, or not. Societies may raise standards of living, or collapse. Cain nations may be able to move beyond the foolishness of warfare and beat their cruise missiles, stealth bombers, WMDs, Apache helicopters, suicide bombs, fighter jets, assault weapons, and cluster explosives into plowshares, or not. But in God's *kairos* time, with or without the existence of *Homo sapiens,* the astounding enterprise called life will go on in God's universe. This is the mission God is on.

Martin Luther (1483–1546), an important figure in the story of Christianity, taught a theology of the cross that contrasts with a theology of glory. A theology of the cross embraces reality. It does body counts. It doesn't hide behind cowardice. Yes, the ravages of Takerism are unforgiveable. Yes, it appears Cain's ability to fix the damage is almost nil. And whether Abel will arise, who knows? But this is the reality before the world, and Christians are called to face it. Rather than de-evolving into positive thinking, optimism, sugarcoating, or Pollyanna naïveté, followers of Jesus Christ meet reality head-on. Actually, forgiveness and reconciliation frees us to do this.

But along with advocating the ability to face truth, Martin Luther's theology of the cross also works to draw us into the deeper reality of God's being and action. With eyes wide open, and our hearts broken by what we see, we are also drawn into the mystery of God's reality, a reality drenched in hope. In the *kairos* of God, the Creator's creation evolves and changes through the eons, eras, periods, and epochs of history. In the *kairos* of God, "God was in Christ reconciling the world unto himself, not counting the trespasses against them" (2 Corinthians 5:19). In *kairos* time, "Jesus came and proclaimed peace to you who were far off and peace to those who were near," so that "you are no longer strangers and aliens, but you are citizens with the saints and also members of the household of God" (Ephesians 2:17, 19), which includes the community of life. In the *kairos* of God, even Cain's rebellion is not beyond recovery.

So a Christian works for peace. A Christian follows Abel of Nazareth and lives as though the world actually belongs to God and the whole community of life. A Christian enters a restored life with the tools of resistance always being wielded with bold, nonviolent persistence. A Christian joins a community in living out a very old but reconsidered, reframed, and renewed mega narrative. A Christian follows Jesus into a community steeped in and in love with sustainable living.

A summary and a call to faithfulness

- Earth life is ancient and evolving; discover and re-enter the process.

- Death is part of life; neither hoard life nor cower in fear of losing it.

- You are created in the image of God *and* in the image of all other Earth creatures; cherish both unreservedly.

- Humans belong to a pioneer species; don't squander this privilege.

- We are not separate from, superior to, the rulers of, or the reason for God's garden; be welcomed back into God's family.

- The biblical Fall is recent rather than original; celebrate this as a release from inevitable destruction.

- Abel's story is grounded in garden wisdom; learn it and live it.

- God is renewing the Earth; be a part of the restoration.

- Jesus Christ can heal both Cain and Abel; do not settle for your "sickness unto death," as Søren Kierkegaard (1813–1855) put it.

- The bustling life forms of Earth are our neighbors; when you till it, keep it with care.

- The Creator loves this world, including you; praise God from whom all blessings flow.

Bibliography

Agel, Jerome B. *We, the People: Great Documents of the American Nation.* New York: Barnes & Noble, Inc., 2000.

Allaby, Michael. *Earth: A Visual Guide.* New York: Metro Books, 2008.

Ayala, Francisco J. *Darwin's Gift to Science and Religion.* Washington, DC: Joseph Henry Press, 2007.

Ballantine, Betty, and Ian Ballantine, ed. *The Native Americans: An Illustrated History.* North Dighton, MA: World Publications Group, Inc., 2001.

Billman, Kathleen D., and Daniel L. Migliore. *Rachel's Cry: Prayer of Lament and Rebirth of Hope.* Cleveland, OH: United Church, 1999.

Bonhoeffer, Dietrich. *Ethics.* New York: MacMillan, 1955.

Borg, Marcus, and N. T. Wright. *The Meaning of Jesus: Two Visions.* San Francisco: HarperSanFrancisco, 1999.

Brueggemann, Walter. "The Liturgy of Abundance, the Myth of Scarcity: Consumerism and Religious Life."

———. *The Prophetic Imagination.* Minneapolis, MN: Augsburg Fortress Press, 2001.

Campbell, Charles L. *The Word Before the Powers: An Ethic of Preaching.* Louisville, KY: Westminster John Knox Press, 2002.

Carmichael, Leonard, ed. *Vanishing Peoples of the Earth.* National Geographic Society, 1968.

Claiborne, Shane. *The Irresistible Revolution: Living as an Ordinary Radical.* Grand Rapids, MI: Zondervan, 2006. www.awip.us and www.thesimpleway.org

DeSalle, Rob, and Ian Tattersall. *Human Origins: What Bones and Genomes Tell Us About Ourselves.* College Station, TX: Texas A&M University Press, 2008.

Diamond, Jared. *Collapse: How Societies Choose to Fail or Succeed.* New York: Penguin Group, 2005.

_____. *Guns, Germs, and Steel: The Fates of Human Societies.* New York: W. W. Norton & Company, 1999.

Egan, Timothy. *The Worst Hard Time: The Untold Story of Those Who Survived the Great American Dust Bowl.* New York: Houghton Mifflin Company, 2006.

Erlander, Daniel. *Manna and Mercy: A Brief History of God's Unfolding Promise to Mend the Entire Universe.* Minneapolis, MN: Augsburg Fortress Press, 1992. www.danielerlander.com

Fenton, Tom. *Bad News: The Decline of Reporting, the Business of News, and the Danger to Us All.* Los Angeles: Regan Books, 2005.

Friedman, Edwin. *Generation to Generation: Family Process in Church and Synagogue.* New York: Guilford Press, 1985.

Fox, Matthew. *Original Blessing: A Primer in Creation Spirituality.* Santa Fe, NM: Bear & Company, Inc., 1983.

Gibbons, Ann. *The First Human: The Race to Discover Our Earliest Ancestors.* New York: Anchor Books, 2006.

Gilbert, Roberta M. *Extraordinary Relationships: A New Way of Thinking About Human Relationships.* New York: John Wiley & Sons, Inc., 1992.

Gould, Stephen Jay, ed. *The Book of Life: An Illustrated History of the Evolution of Life on Earth.* New York: W. W. Norton & Company, 2001.

Heinberg, Richard. *The Party's Over: Oil, War and the Fate of Industrial Societies.* Gabriola Island, BC: New Society Publishers, 2003.

Kline, Benjamine. *First Alone the River: A Brief History of the U.S. Environmental Movement.* Lanham, MD: Rowan & Littlefield Publishers, Inc., 2007.

Lakoff, George. *Don't Think of an Elephant!: Know Your Values and Frame the Debate.* White River Junction, VT: Chelsea Green Publishing, 2004.

Levine, Amy-Jill. *The Historical Jesus in Context.* Princeton, NJ: Princeton University Press, 2006.

_____. *The Misunderstood Jew: The Church and the Scandal of the Jewish Jesus.* San Francisco: HarperSanFrancisco, 2006.

McFague, Sallie. *Super, Natural Christians: How We Should Love Nature.* Minneapolis: Augsburg Fortress Press, 1997.

McLaren, Brian D. *Everything Must Change: Jesus, Global Crisis, and a Revolution of Hope.* Nashville TN: Thomas Nelson, 2007. www.brianmclaren.net

_____. *The Last Word and the Word After That: A Tale of Faith, Doubt, and a New Kind of Christianity.* San Francisco, CA: Jossey-Bass, 2005.

Meyers, Ched. *Binding the Strong Man*. Maryknoll, NY: Orbis Books, 1988.

_____. *Say to This Mountain: Mark's Story of Discipleship*. Maryknoll, NY: Orbis Books, 1996.

Miller, William Lee. *President Lincoln: The Duty of a Statesman*. New York: Alfred A. Knopf, 2008.

Mix, Lucas John. *Life in Space: Astrobiology for Everyone*. Cambridge, MA: Harvard University Press, 2009.

Morell, Virginia. "Inside Animal Minds." *National Geographic*. (March 2008): 36–61.

Niebuhr, Reinhold. *The Irony of American History*. Chicago: University of Chicago Press, 1952.

Palmer, Douglas. *Prehistoric Past Revealed: The Four Billion Year History of Life on Earth*. Berkeley, CA: University of California Press, 2003.

Peters, Ted. *The Stem Cell Debate*. Minneapolis: Fortress Press, 2007.

Pollan, Michael. *In Defense of Food*. New York: The Penguin Press, 2008.

_____. *The Omnivore's Dilemma: A Natural History of Four Meals*. New York: The Penguin Press, 2006.

Prescott, Roger. *Day by Day: Seeing the Sacred in Everyday Life*. Lima, OH: Fairway Press, 2008.

Quinn, Daniel. *Beyond Civilization: Humanity's Next Great Adventure*. New York: Three Rivers, 1999. www.ishmael.org

_____. *Ishmael: An Adventure of the Mind and Spirit*. New York: Bantam Books, 1992.

_____. *My Ishmael*. New York: Bantam Books, 1997.

_____. *The Story of B: An Adventure of the Mind and Spirit*. New York: Bantam Books, 1996.

Roberts, J. Deotis. *Bonhoeffer and King: Speaking the Truth to Power*. Louisville, KY: Westminster John Knox Press, 2005.

Roberts, Paul. *The End of Food*. New York: Houghton Mifflin Harcourt, 2008.

Rollins, Peter. *The Fidelity of Betrayal: Towards a Church Beyond Belief*. Brewster, MA: Paraclete Press, 2008.

_____. *How (Not) to Speak of God*. Brewster, MA: Paraclete Press, 2006.

Rossing, Barbara R. *The Rapture Exposed: The Message of Hope in the Book of Revelation*. Boulder, CO: Westview Press, 2004.

Sheridan, Thomas E., and Nancy J. Prezo, eds. *Paths of Life: American Indians of the Southwest and Northern Mexico*. Tucson, AZ: The University of Arizona Press, 1996.

Speth, James Gustave. *The Bridge at the Edge of the World*. New Haven, CT: Yale University Press, 2008.

Spong, John Shelby. *Why Christianity Must Change or Die: A Bishop Speaks to Believers in Exile*. San Francisco: HarperSanFrancisco, 1998.

Stix, Gary. "Traces of a Distant Past." *Scientific American* (July 2008).

Stringer, Curtis, and Peter Andrews. *The Complete World of Human Evolution*. Devon, England: Thames & Hudson, 2005.

Taylor, Barbara Brown. *Leaving Church: A Memoir of Faith*. San Francisco: Harper, 2006. www.barbarabrowntaylor.com

_____. *The Luminous Web: Essays On Science and Religion*. Cambridge, MA: Cowley Publications, 2000.

Tutu, Desmond. *No Future Without Forgiveness*. New York: Doubleday, 1999.

Van Huyssteen, J. Wentzel. *Alone in the World? Human Uniqueness in Science and Theology*. Grand Rapids, MI: Wm. B. Eerdmans Publishing Co., 2006.

Waldman, Carl. *Atlas of the North American Indian*. New York: Facts on File, Inc., 2009.

Wiesel, Elie. *Night*. New York: Hill and Wang, 2006.

Young, William Paul. *The Shack: Where Tragedy Confronts Eternity*. Newbury Park, CA: Windblown Media, 2007.

Appendix A

Biblical Interpretation

My Christian tradition (Evangelical Lutheran Church in America) cherishes the scriptures of our faith. We believe they are the written word of God inspired by God's Holy Spirit speaking through the enfleshed and contextualized lives of its storytellers and authors. Through these written scriptures, in many cases growing out of prior and often fluid oral traditions, God speaks to us to create and sustain faith and fellowship for radical servant living in God's world today and eternal life after we die.

However, we also note an important distinction between what is known as "scripture," and what we call the "message" held within it; between "Bible," and the "living Word" found in the Bible. While not to be separated, it is *idolatry* to make them one. Several images are helpful to consider:

Manger: Martin Luther (1483–1546) once used the image of a manger holding the Christ Child as a way to think of the Bible. The manger is the Bible. It holds the Christ. Yes, go to the manger/Bible to meet the living Word/Christ. You will find him revealed there more clearly than in any other writings on Earth. But you will also find other things in the manger, such as wood, straw, and manure. Don't mistake this container of Christ for the Christ. Don't make the manger and the Christ one and the same. This is idolatry and will give a distorted (dare I say Taker?) view of life.

Cracked pot: St. Paul invoked another image: "We have this *treasure* in *Earthen vessels,* so that it may be made clear that this extraordinary power belongs to God and does not come from us" (2 Corinthians 4:7, emphasis added). The Bible is the "Earthen vessel" (clay jar, cracked pot), which holds the "treasure" (living Word, Christ.) The Earthen vessel is not the treasure. Christ is. Don't mix them up.

The danger of pedestals: When we humans cherish people or things, we sometimes put them on pedestals. We assume we are honoring what we've put on a pedestal (a parent, a girlfriend, a president, a child, a pastor, the Virgin Mary, scripture, etc.). Actually, the exact opposite happens. We dishonor them. Placing people on pedestals is a form of control, of putting someone or something on a shelf or in a box. It's one way of keeping someone or something at a safe distance. We idealize them and take away their humanity, that which makes them real. Christians are impoverished when they put the scriptures, or even Jesus, on a pedestal.

Mining for gold: Each week the preacher immerses herself in the text, in life, in study, in the community of faith, in the community of life, in prayer. The week begins with dead words on paper. The aim is to live those words and to "mine" those words (as one would "mine" rock to find gold) in such a way that the living Word/Christ rises and is encountered. This living Word/Christ is what needs to be preached on Sunday. The living Word does not equal the words on the page no matter how eloquently or piously or loudly they are orated.

Incarnate word: As humans we don't have access to the "pure" word of God in its written form. We only have access to the "incarnate" (enfleshed) word of God in its written form. We only have access to the word of God/treasure as it comes to us through the wonder and messiness of flesh and Earthy context (preacher, Bible, sacraments, manger, prayer, Earthen vessel, etc.). The good news is that God has made such an enfleshed word sufficient. This, in fact, is the "high" view of scripture, perhaps in a similar way to the cross being Jesus' time of real "glory." However, the all too common rejection of this incarnate word in favor of "purity," which is never attained but all too often claimed, in the end produces only a lowest common denominator Phariseeism. Pseudo-Christianity. This very common and popular false "Christianity" kills, unlike true Christian faith and living, which gives life.

John the Baptist: The relationship between Jesus and John the Baptizer is instructive. John, like the Bible, came "as a witness to testify to the light. He was not the light, but he came to testify to the light" (John 1:7–8). John, like the Bible, points to Christ. "Here is the Lamb of God who takes away the sin of the world" (John 1:29). And further, John, like the Bible, knows he is not the important one: "He must increase, but I must decrease" (John 3:30). John the Baptizer is very important to the Christian faith. But we obviously miss the point if we "worship" John, or assign divinity to John, or think of John as the way and the truth and the life. John's task is to point beyond himself. So with scripture.

Dogs: My family had a pet dog named Hershey for thirteen years. If we pointed toward something and said words such as, "Hey, look at that squirrel," or, "See that piece of food on the floor?" or, "Go lay down," Hershey would look at and start licking our pointing finger rather that what the finger was pointing toward. Such is the fundamentalist/literalist approach to scripture. Obsessed with the pointing finger, it misses what it is pointing toward.

Appendix B

Cain Invades South America, 1532 CE

The Spanish Conquistadors visited terror upon the Inca families in the Andes Mountains of South America. The following is an actual account written by eyewitnesses, which is woven together and quoted in Jared Diamond's extensive anthropological and historical book *Guns, Germs, and Steel*.[123] The year is 1532, as several Spaniards put pen to paper:

> The prudence, fortitude, military discipline, labors, perilous navigations, and battles of the Spaniards—vassals of the most invincible Emperor of the Roman Catholic Empire, our natural King and Lord—will cause joy to the faithful and terror to the infidels. For this reason, and for the glory of God our Lord and for the service of the Catholic imperial Majesty, it has seemed good to me to write this narrative, and to send it to Your Majesty, that all may have a knowledge of what is here related. It will be to the glory of God, because

---

123. From *Guns, Germs, and Steel: The Fates of Human Societies* by Jared Diamond. Copyright © 1997 by Jared Diamond. Used by permission of W. W. Norton & Company, Inc., 69–77.

they have conquered and brought to our holy Catholic Faith so vast a number of heathens, aided by His holy guidance. It will be to the honor of our Emperor because, by reason of his great power and good fortune, such events happened in his time. It will give joy to the faithful that such battles have been won, such provinces discovered and conquered, such riches brought home for the King and for themselves; and that such terror has been spread among the infidels, such admiration excited in all mankind.

For when, either in ancient or modern times, have such great exploits been achieved by so few against so many, over so many, over so many climes, across so many seas, over such distances by land, to subdue the unseen and unknown? Whose deeds can be compared with those of Spain? Our Spaniards, being few in number, never having more than 200 or 300 men together, and sometimes only 100 and even fewer, have, in our times, conquered more territory than has ever been known before, or than all the faithful and infidel princes possess. I will only write, at present, or what befell in the conquest, and I will not write much, in order to avoid prolixity.

Governor Pizarro wished to obtain intelligence from some Indians who had come from Cajamarca, so he had them tortured. They confessed that they had heard that Atahuallpa was waiting for the Governor at Cajamarca. The Governor then ordered us to advance. On reading the entrance to Cajamarca, we saw the camp of Atahuallpa at a distance of a league, in the skirts of the mountains. The Indians' camp looked like a very beautiful city. They had so many tents that we were all filled with great apprehension. Until then, we had never seen anything like this in the Indies. It filled all our Spaniards with fear and confusion. But we could not show any fear or turn back, for if the Indians had sensed any weakness in us, even the Indians that we were bringing with us as guides would have killed us. So we made a show of good spirits, and after carefully observing the town and the tents, we descended into the valley and entered Cajamarca.

We talked a lot among ourselves about what to do. All of us were full of fear, because we were so few in number and we had penetrated so far into a land where we could not hope to receive reinforcements. We all met with the Governor to debate what we should undertake the next day. Few of us slept that night, and we kept watch in the square of Cajamarca, looking at the campfires of the Indian army. It was a frightening sight. Most of the campfires were on a hillside and so close to each other that it looked like the sky brightly studded with stars. There was no distinction that night between the mighty and the lowly, or between foot soldiers and horsemen. Everyone carried out sentry duty fully armed. So too did the good old Governor, who went about encouraging his men. The Governor's brother Hernando Pizarro estimated the number of Indian soldiers there at 40,000, but he was telling a lie just to encourage us, for there were actually more than 80,000 Indians.

On the next morning a messenger from Atahuallpa arrived, and the Governor said to him, "Tell your lord to come when and how he pleases, and that, in what way soever he may come I will receive him as a friend and brother. I pray that he may come quickly, for I desire to see him. No harm or insult will befall him."

The Governor concealed his troops around the square at Cajamarca, dividing the cavalry into two portions of which he gave the command of one to his brother Hernando Pizarro and the command of the other to Hernando de Soto. In like manner he divided the infantry, he himself taking one part and giving the other to his brother Juan Pizarro. At the same time, he ordered Pedro de Candia with two or three infantrymen to go with trumpets to a small fort in the plaza and to station themselves there with a small piece of artillery. When all the Indians, and Atahuallpa with them, had entered the Plaza, the Governor would give a signal to

Candia and his men, after which they should start firing the gun, and the trumpets should sound, and at the sound of the trumpets the cavalry should dash out of the large court where they were waiting hidden in readiness.

At noon Atahuallpa began to draw up his men and to approach. Soon we saw the entire plain full of Indians, halting periodically to wait for more Indians who kept filing out of the camp behind them. They kept filing out in separate detachments into the afternoon. The four detachments were now close to our camp, and still more troops kept issuing from the camp of the Indians. In front of Atahuallpa went 2,000 Indians who swept the road ahead of him, and these were followed by the warriors, half of whom were marching in the fields on one side of him and half on the other side.

First came a squadron of Indians dressed in clothes of different colors, like a chessboard. They advanced, removing the straws from the ground and sweeping the road. Next came three squadrons in different dresses, dancing and singing. Then came a number of men with armor, large metal plates, and crowns of gold and silver. So great was the amount of furniture of gold and silver which they bore, that it was a marvel to observe how the sun glinted upon it. Among them came the figure of Atahuallpa in a very fine litter with the ends of its timbers covered in silver. Eighty lords carried him on their shoulders, all wearing a very rich blue livery. Atahuallpa himself was very richly dressed, with his crowns on his head and a collar of large emeralds around his neck. He sat on a small stool with a rich saddle cushion resting on his litter. The litter was lined with parrot feathers of many colors and decorated with plates of gold and silver.

Behind Atahuallpa came two other litters and two hammocks, in which were some high chiefs, then several squadrons of Indians with crowns of gold and silver. These Indian squadrons began to enter the plaza to the accompaniment of great songs, and thus entering they occupied every part of the plaza. In the meantime all of us Spaniards were waiting ready, hidden in a courtyard, full of fear. Many of us urinated without noticing it, out of sheer terror. On reaching the center of the plaza, Atahuallpa remained in his litter on high, while his troops continued to file in behind him.

Governor Pizarro now sent Friar Vincent de Valverde to go speak to Atahuallpa, and to require Atahuallpa in the name of God and of the King of Spain that Atahuallpa subject himself to the law of our Lord Jesus Christ and to the service of His Majesty the King of Spain. Advancing with a cross in one hand and the Bible in the other hand, and going among Indian troops up to the place where Atahuallpa was, the Friar thus addressed him: "I am Priest of God, and I teach Christians the things of God, and in like manner I come to teach you. What I teach is that which God says to us in this Book. Therefore, on the part of God and of the Christians, I beseech you to be their friend, for such is God's will, and it will be for your good.

Atahuallpa asked for the Book, that he might look at it, and the Friar gave it to him closed. Atahuallpa did not know how to open the Book, and the Friar was extending his arm to do so, when Atahuallpa, in great anger, gave him a blow on the arm, not wishing that it should be opened. Then he opened it himself, and, without any astonishment at the letters and paper he threw it away from him five or six paces, his face a deep crimson.

The Friar returned to Pizarro, shouting, "Come out! Come out, Christians! Come at these enemy dogs who reject the things of God. That tyrant has thrown my book of holy law to the ground! Did you not see what happened? Why remain polite and servile toward this over-proud dog when the plains are full of Indians? March out against him, for I absolve you!"

The Governor then gave the signal to Candia, who began to fire off the guns. At the same time the trumpets were sounded, and the armored Spanish troops, both cavalry and infantry, sallied forth out of their hiding places straight into the mass of unarmed Indians crowding the square, giving the Spanish battle cry, "Santiago!" We had placed rattles on the horses to terrify the Indians. The booming of the guns, the blowing of the trumpets, and the rattles on the horses threw the Indians into panicked confusion. The Spaniards fell upon them and began to cut them to pieces. The Indians were so filled with fear that they climbed on top of one another, formed mounds, and suffocated each other. Since they were unarmed, they were attacked without danger to any Christian. The cavalry rode them down, killing and wounding, and following in pursuit. The infantry made so good an assault on those that remained that in a short time most of them were put to the sword.

The Governor himself took his sword and dagger, entered the thick of the Indians with the Spaniards who were with him, and with great bravery reached Atahuallpa's litter. He fearlessly grabbed Atahuallpa's left arm and shouted "Santiago!", but he could not pull Atahuallpa out of his litter because it was held up high. Although we killed the Indians who held the litter, others at once took their places and held it aloft, and in this manner we spent a long time in overcoming and killing Indians. Finally seven or eight Spaniards on horseback spurred on their horses, rushed upon the litter from one side, and with great effort they heaved it over on its side. In that way Atahuallpa was captured, and the Governor took Atahuallpa to his lodging. The Indians carrying the litter, and those escorting Atahuallpa, never abandoned him: all died around him.

The panic-stricken Indians remaining in the square, terrified at the firings of the guns and at the horses—something they had never seen—tried to flee from the square by knocking down a stretch of all and running out onto the plain outside. Our cavalry jumped the broken wall and charged into the plain, shouting, "Chase those with the fancy clothes! Don't let any escape! Spear them!" All of the other Indian soldiers whom Atahuallpa had brought were a mile from Cajamarca ready for battle, but not one made a move, and during all this not one Indian raised a weapon against a Spaniard. When the squadrons of Indians who had remained in the plain outside the town saw the other Indians fleeing and shouting, most of them too panicked and fled. It was an astonishing sight, for the whole valley for 15 or 20 miles was completely filled with Indians. Night had already fallen, and our cavalry were continuing to spear Indians in the fields, when we heard a trumpet calling for us to reassemble at camp.

If night had not come on, few out of the more than 40,000 Indian troops would have been left alive. Six or seven thousand Indians lay dead, and many more had their arms cut off and other wounds. Atahuallpa himself admitted that we had killed 7,000 of his men in that battle. The man killed in one of the litters was his minister, the lord of Chincha, of whom he was very fond. All those Indians who bore Atahuallpa's litter appeared to be high chiefs and councilors. They were all killed, as well as those Indians who were carried in the other litters and hammocks. The lord of Cajamarca was also killed, and others, but their numbers were so great that they could not be counted, for all who came in attendance of Atahuallpa were great lords. It was extraordinary to see so powerful a ruler captured in so short a time, when he had come with such a mighty army. Truly, it was not accomplished by our own forces, for there were so few of us. It was by the grace of God, which is great.

Atahuallpa's robes had been torn off when the Spaniards pulled him out of his litter. The Governor ordered clothes to be brought to him, and when Atahuallpa was dressed, the Governor ordered Atahuallpa to sit near him and soothed his rage and agitation at finding himself so quickly fallen from his high estate. The Governor said to Atahuallpa, "Do not take it as an insult that you have been defeated and taken prisoner, for with the Christians who come with me, though so few in number, I have conquered greater king-doms than yours, and have defeated other more powerful lords than you, imposing upon them the dominion of the Emperor, whose vassal I am, and who is King of Spain and of the universal world. We come to conquer this land by his command, that all may come to the knowledge of God and of His Holy Catholic Faith; and by reason of our good mission, God, the Creator of heaven and Earth and of all things in them, permits this, in order that you may know Him and come out from the bestial and diabolical life that you lead. It is for this reason that we, being so few in number, subju-gate that vast host. When you have seen the errors in which you live, you will understand the good that we have done you by coming to your land by order of his Majesty the King of Spain. Our Lord permitted that your people should be brought low and that no Indian should be able to offend a Christian.

These centuries-old accounts were compiled by Jared Diamond. It is hard to imagine that such thought processes and behavior could have even remotely been associated with the life, teachings, actions, crucifixion, death, and resurrection of Jesus of Nazareth and Jesus the Christ.

Appendix C

Sermon on the Parable of the Wedding Banquet

October 12, 2008 • 22nd Sunday after Pentecost

Matthew 22:1–14 • Rev. Jen Rude

Resurrection Lutheran Church, Chicago

More than once this week someone said to me, "I need some good news. Our economy is failing, days are getting shorter and darker, jobs are scarce or threatened. I need some good news." Perhaps that's why some of you came to worship this morning. And then we look at the parable this week. And we are still left needing some good news.

A parable by definition is a riddle, puzzle, layered story. It *should* be confusing and difficult, and this one lives up to that promise.

But sometimes we move too quickly past the confused stage and too easily get into a rut with our biblical parables, and automatically allegorize them. We read that the king represents

God, the wedding banquet represents the marriage between Christ and the church, those invited first represent the religious leaders and elite, and on and on.

But sometimes we can't ignore a confusing or difficult part, and something forces us to reconsider, to rework the puzzle, and to wonder if we've got the right picture.

I pray that you would be patient and open as we move through the parable this morning, exploring some of these difficult pieces, and as we look at the parable in perhaps some ways that differ from those you have heard or thought of before. I recognize that I'm the one with the microphone, and that might be unfair. But I hope, as always, that we can be in conversation together about scripture and the ways we hear God speaking to us.

So back to this challenging text. I imagine I'm not the only one disturbed by a God as king who murders those who don't come to the banquet, who destroys their city, and who casts out those with improper attire into the darkness with weeping and gnashing of teeth.

And so I wonder why we have always made the king into God. What if Jesus is getting at something entirely different in this parable? What if the king is *not* God or Jesus?

"The kingdom of heaven may be compared to a king," the parable begins. The Greek reads more accurately, "a man, a king," perhaps to tip us off that we shouldn't so quickly divinize this king.

We people in twenty-first century United States hear the parable and don't have an immediate image of a king, so maybe that's one reason we often jump to the allegorical reading where the king represents God or Jesus and ignore or rationalize away the king's tyrannical violence or make that symbolic, too. If the parable began, "there was a president," we would have a picture in our mind. Kings, though, are a stretch for us. Perhaps we also jump to Jesus as king because we kind of like that image; we want a kingly Jesus who will take care of business and set things right.

But Jesus' audience didn't have to imagine a king. They

knew a king. King Herod. Perhaps you've heard of him before! He threw a banquet earlier in Matthew's gospel.

Banquets thrown by kings were common. But they were often used as a tactic of control, demanding obedience and loyalty under the guise of festivities and free food. Come, I'll feed you and entertain you, but I will demand your devotion, your submission, your very selves. But saying no to such an "invitation" was dangerous, as we learn.

The wedding banquet invitation goes out. But those invited would not come. So the king tries again, sending slaves, saying, "Look, I have prepared my dinner, my oxen and my fat calves have been slaughtered, and everything is ready; come to the banquet." We obviously know that the king himself did not prepare the banquet, but notice the first person language: *I* have prepared *my* fat calves. The personal nature of this invitation cannot be missed: not coming is a personal insult.

But those invited made light of it and went away. Did they realize what their refusal meant?

But really, who wouldn't want to go to a wedding banquet? Well, let's look a little deeper. Just a few chapters back, king Herod threw a banquet party. And he ended up serving John the Baptist's head on a platter!

The people knew that king's banquets were not always pleasant, or safe, affairs.

So when invited, they responded with "Thanks, but no thanks." But the king doesn't take no lightly. He sends out his slaves to reinvite the people. And the people who have turned down the invitation seize the slaves of the king and mistreat them, killing them. One has to wonder what all came before such an act of violence? That the people would choose violence over attending a banquet clues us in to the deeper and darker parts of the king, and the parable.

Upon hearing the news of the violence, the king was enraged! So he sent troops to destroy them and to burn their city.

And then, still obsessed with an empty wedding hall, the king sends out his slaves to invite anyone they can find on the streets. He doesn't care who it is, but the wedding banquet must be full! This is about pride and honor. Notice the bride and groom never even make an appearance in the parable. This is about the king. "Go therefore into the main streets, and invite everyone you find to the wedding banquet."

And the slaves head to the street and seemingly find plenty of people to fill the hall. That's not hard to imagine, considering that their city was being burned all around them, and perhaps there was no place to go other than the streets. Surrounded by fire and ash, having seen those who refused to attend killed, this *invitation* sounds anything but invitational. And so the people go.

It's an ugly and disturbing scene. So where do we find Jesus in the midst of this craziness, death, violence, and hopelessness?

We could ask such a question today, in this often ugly and disturbing scene of our world. Where do we find Jesus, as our economy tumbles, as violence in schools increases, and homelessness rages, as war drags on, and illness plagues us?

The parable begins with, "the kingdom of heaven," so we imagine Jesus must be present in this parable. But if he is not the king, then *who* is he?

There is one character in the parable who does not fit into the scene, one who is causing problems for the king, one who ruffles the feathers of the king when he remains silent in the face of accusation, one who refuses to respond to violence with violence and one who suffers the consequences of such a bold stance: *the man without the wedding robe*.

Could this be Jesus?

He comes to the banquet to be with others who certainly had no choice, but he refuses to be clothed with the king's garment. This quiet response foreshadows Jesus' standing accused before Pilate. Scripture tells us, "He gave them no answer, not even to a single charge, so that the governor was greatly amazed." And Jesus bears the consequences of not participating in the royal and religious establishment of power. He is cast out of the banquet into the darkness of death.

In Matthew's gospel by this point we are journeying quickly

toward Jesus' end, a crucifixion marked with a posting "King of the Jews" above his head, a title reserved for another king, King Herod.

This challenge to the king and powers is what got Jesus killed. But Jesus as king says no to this banquet of false generosity and real control, no to this king of manipulation and violence. And we know denying both "invitations" is risky—and it may get you killed.

The invitations for us to participate in the king's banquet are persistent; we are constantly bombarded with promises to make our lives easier, to give us more power, to fill our bellies and pocketbooks. And perhaps we, too, fear saying no. Fear is a powerful tool. The king knows that.

But ultimately, this banquet is a banquet of death: of ourselves, of our neighbor, and of our world.

But perhaps this unrobed man knows what Jesus knows, that this king of death will not have the last word. Because, finally, here I believe is precisely the good news. *There is another banquet.*

Isaiah envisions for us a different banquet: "On this mountain the LORD of hosts will make for all peoples a feast of rich food, a feast of well-aged wines, of rich food filled with marrow, of well-aged wines strained clear. And he will destroy on this mountain the shroud that is cast over all peoples, the sheet that is spread over all nations; he will swallow up death forever."

This is a banquet of abundance, an invitation to life.

Attending this banquet requires removing the shroud, the sheet, the robe that has us blind to the one from whose table we are eating and who we are consuming.

And then we will truly be able to see the banquet of the kingdom of heaven, and the One who feeds us the food of life.

We are all invited to God's banquet. But if we are too busy eating at the king's table, we might not even realize that we are still starving, or that the food we are eating is rotten.

There is another banquet. And all are invited to this banquet today. And always. If the economy falls apart, we will still gather to eat and drink and receive blessing. If this building falls down, we will still gather to eat and drink and receive blessing. If your own life crumbles around you, we will still gather. And if you cannot bring yourself to come and eat, we will save you a place.

Hear the good news. All are invited. Come, clothe yourselves in the kingdom of heaven. Come, take your place at the banquet table of God.

Appendix D

Group Discussion Questions

1. Do you agree that the Christian story needs to be reconsidered?

2. What do you think of the assessment that members of *Homo sapiens* are seriously damaging God's Earth?

3. In your view, is it possible to reframe the Christian story without destroying it?

4. Initially, with which of the main ideas listed on pages **6** and **7** do you agree and disagree?

5. How do you understand the Creator's intentions for the world, for humanity?

1. Why do you think God's cosmos is so vast?

2. Why do you think God began to create?

3. How would you describe or define life?

Chapter 2. 17

1. What do you think of the notion that God's evolving garden never was utopia, i.e., a perfect Eden paradise?

2. Which provisions of life in the list on page **17** would you agree are normal and necessary?

3. How does a food chain fit your view of God's garden?

4. How does the principal of balance fit in?

5. What is meant by the "terrifying power" of the Tree of the Knowledge of Good and Evil?

6. Do you think of God as a being who interacts with creation?

Chapter 3. 21

1. Does this summary of humanity's evolution fit your understanding?

2. Compare "survival of the fittest" thinking with survival of those species that "fit in."

3. Can you picture families, clans, tribes, and communities of *Homo sapiens* spreading around the Earth for 200,000 years? What do you think it would it have been like to live then?

4. What do you think of the notion of *Homo sapiens* being a pioneer or trailblazer species, rather than the crown or end of creation?

5. Do you agree that humans are underdeveloped in some areas, compared to other species?

6. What makes sense and doesn't make sense about the suggestion that humans are created in both the image of God *and* in the image of plants and animals and soil?

7. Respond to the farmer's comment, "The farther humans get away from the dirt, the crazier they become."

8. Do you agree that the garden doesn't need humans?

9. How do you understand "dominion"? Is it a helpful word, or not?

10. Can the notion of an evolving Tree of Life be compatible with the notion of a creator God?

11. How does evolving life find balance between variety and homogeneity?

12. What does it mean to "neither romanticize nor demonize" our *Homo sapiens* ancestors (and there predecessor species)?

13. Is death natural and intended by God? Do you see a difference between cherishing life and hoarding it?

1. In writing the Christian creeds in the third and fourth centuries CE, the authors left out both the Fall and the life of Jesus. Why do you think they did this?

2. How do you understand the Fall?

3. How do you understand Original Sin? Original Blessing?

4. Do you think Adam and Eve were the actual first parents of humanity?

5. Would you agree with Daniel Erlander's portrayal of human sin as people "acting like big deals"?

1. "God as presiding minister of Creation": what is appealing or disagreeable about this image?

2. How is evil a new thing in this reconsideration of the Christian story?

3. Do you find it helpful or confusing to think that the Fall story refers to actual changes that began spreading 6,000 to 10,000 years ago, that the biblical storytellers were beginning to experience in their own time and place?

4. What do you think about human exceptionalism? About the Protagoras and Francis Bacon quotations?

5. What changes occur when humans start to think of the garden as an enemy, or untamed jungle?

6. Is the Fall really a mutiny, or something else?

7. Explore the difference between sustainable agriculture (or horticulture) and totalitarian agriculture.

8. Discuss the implications of Daniel Quinn's terms "Leavers" and "Takers."

9. How did "locking up food" change garden life for humans?

10. Did you know human misbehavior brings to extinction over eighty species each day?

1. Are we humans "in over our heads" when we try to rule the Earth?

2. Describe Cain's worldview.

3. Describe Abel's worldview.

4. What do you think of the notion of indigenous peoples being identified as Abel?

5. Did God ban humanity from the Tree of the Knowledge of Good and Evil to test obedience, or to protect creation?

6. Was God in the main happy with *Homo sapiens* during the first 200,000 years of evolving existence prior to Cain's mutiny?

7. What do you think of the Conquistadors represented in appendix B (page **193**)?

8. Should we refrain from criticizing historical figures? Is it ever appropriate to use words like "genocide" to describe their behavior?

9. Should other creatures fear humans who live Cain's way?

10. How many humans can live in the garden in a sustainable way in your locale? Is your community nearing a breaking point, or not?

11. Is the problem too many people, or how consumer peoples live? Or both?

12. With which of Cain's defenses and rationalizations do you agree (page **65**)?

13. Are Cain's values mainstream in our culture? Nation? In your family? Among your friends?

Chapter 7 69

1. What do you think of the notion "addicted to prosperity"?

2. Are we trapped in an economic system where we "must expand in order to keep from collapsing"?

3. What do you think of a nation that plans to use weapons of mass destruction?

Chapter 8. 73

1. Are Cain nations fighting Cain nations today?

2. Are you familiar with Jabba the Hutt from the movie *Star Wars*? What works and doesn't work about this metaphor?

3. Comment on the role of entertainment in furthering Jabba's or Cain's goals.

4. How is and isn't the military an arm of Cain?

5. Does the "military-industrial complex" play a role in promoting warfare as a tool of governance?

6. Does the news media?

7. The notion that human nature is not ontologically sinful is a radical departure from common understandings in Western Christianity. What are your thoughts?

Chapter 9. 87

1. What do you think of associating the lives and words of prophets, rabbis, sages, and martyrs with calls to live Abel's way of life?

2. How is living in reciprocal relationships within creation different from conquering creation?

3. Do you agree that Cain today suffers from a "nature deficit disorder"?

4. Why do you think Cain persists?

5. Is addiction language useful? Can you think of a better metaphor?

6. Does thinking of Jesus of Nazareth in Abel terms give you new insights into who Jesus was and is?

Chapter 10 93

1. Describe the perfect storm that gave rise to Cain's successful conquest.

2. Discuss Daniel Quinn's idea of the "Great Forgetting."

3. Do you see Creation beginning in 4004 BCE, or 13.7 billion years ago, or at some other time? Does your answer matter or not matter?

4. Were you taught that life prior to 6,000 to 10,000 years ago was inferior, purposeless, and gloomy?

5. What do you think of the Creation Museum in Petersburg, Kentucky?

6. What do you think of the understanding of scripture discussed in appendix A (page **189**)?

7. Do evolutionary scientists belittle pre-Cain life, too? If so, why do they do that?

8. Can you think of examples where you have seen the enactment of Cain's story produce neurosis, dis-ease, and existential disrepair?

9. Why do you think Taker nations are such fertile markets for addictive mood-altering drugs?

10. Do you think God's garden of life is in peril?

11. Do you consider Earth or heaven to be the true home for humanity?

12. What is your understanding of heaven? Of hell?

13. Do you agree that Taker cultures see the Fall actually as a liberation and emancipation?

1. What gaps do you find in this reconsideration?

2. What other objections would you raise?

1. Which author responses to the question "Is there hope?" give you hope?

1. Which possibility for the future seems most likely to you?

2. Do you agree or disagree with the statements on page **132** regarding information, knowledge, and communications technology?

1. Do you think our educational systems in general foster Takerism?

2. Pick a university department or career field. How might those entities get on the side of Abel? Is that desirable? Doable?

3. Is Abel's side losing? Why or why not?

4. Do you agree that many Cains lift up Jesus' name, "but then go on to live private, cultural, and national lives at odds with Jesus' Abel living?"

5. What are your thoughts on our fascination with technology? What is going well? What isn't?

6. Can humans live in reciprocal and mutually beneficial ways with the other creatures of God's garden?

7. Which is easier to accomplish, Cain's narrative or Abel's narrative?

8. Discuss Michael Pollan's recommendation for healthy and responsible eating: "Eat food. Not too much. Mostly plants."

9. Could Abel's way produce an adequate and sustainable economy?

10. Do you think God will give up on humans? Why, or why not?

Chapter 14 149

1. Why do you think Judaism and Christianity came so late in the history of Earth, and so late in human history?

2. Are religions human made, divine made, or some combination of both?

3. What do you think of Daniel Quinn's words about "being saved" on page **154**?

4. With which theory of the atonement do you identify?

5. What do you think the cross event is about?

6. Discuss the "mirror" and "window" metaphors for Jesus' crucifixion.

7. What about the "white blood corpuscle" analogy?

8. What do you think of Desmond Tutu's belief that "there is no future without forgiveness"?

9. Does forgiveness require a restored relationship in order to work?

10. Do assertive but nonviolent word/actions have any power?

1. Which tools of resistance are most important for you?

2. What did you think of Mother Theresa's diary entries?

1. Do you think the apostle Paul and the New Testament writers would embrace current forms of Christianity, or are they the "different gospel" Paul warned us about?

2. What do you think of the notion of reframing? How significant is it?

3. Do you think humans are destroying God's garden? Would having a different story make a difference?

4. Do you generally agree with or disagree with the reconsidered Christian narrative presented in this book?